The Wounds You Didn't Choose

A Journey from Silent Scars to Strength

Robin L O'Brien

DEDICATION PAGE

To my husband Rich, whom God sent to love and heal me. I Love you and thank you for standing by me darling.

And to my daughter Ashley and family, who bring sunshine into my life every single day.

and

**To the ones who were hurt too early, blamed too often,
and silenced too long—
this is for you.
You deserved better, and you deserve healing.**

Table of Contents

OPENING LETTER TO THE READER

Dear Reader,

Before you turn another page, I need you to know something important: **none of this was your fault.** The pain you carry, the questions you still ask, the nights you've cried quietly so no one would hear— those things didn't grow from something broken inside you. They came from moments, people, and environments you didn't choose.

I know what it feels like to grow up believing the hurt was somehow deserved. I know what it's like to love people who leave, trust people who break you, and blame yourself for the choices others made. For a long time, I thought if I had just been "better," or "good enough" maybe my story would have been different.

Maybe your mind has whispered that same lie.

This book is my truth, but parts of it might feel like yours, too. Not because our lives are identical, but because pain has a way of giving strangers the same scars.

What I promise you is this:
I won't rush your healing.

I won't pretend trauma is neat or pretty.
And I won't tell you to "just get over it."

Instead, I'll walk with you through the parts of my
story that shaped me, broke me, and ultimately
rebuilt me. And I hope, somewhere in these
chapters, you find words that your younger self
always needed to hear.

You are safe here.
You are believed here.
You are worthy here.

With love,

Robin L. O'Brien

INTRODUCTION

Introduction: The Unchosen Wounds

Some wounds arrive without warning.
A slammed door.
A raised hand.
A broken promise.
A tiny voice inside you whispering, "Why me?"

For a long time, I believed the pain in my life was a reflection of my worth. If people left me, I must have deserved it. If I was hurt, I must have caused it. If I was crying, I must have been "too sensitive."

But the truth is simple and hard at the same time:

The wounds that shaped me were never mine to justify or carry.

Maybe you've felt that too.

Maybe you were the child who flinched at sudden movements.
The teenager who learned to hide emotions and felt you couldn't let anyone in.
The adult who keeps trying to be "enough" for people who shouldn't need convincing.
The partner who panics when someone they love walks out the door, hoping they will return to only you.

The friend who smiles while quietly falling apart wishing you could be happy too.

This book is my story, yes. But it's also a mirror—reflecting the parts of you that were never protected, never comforted, never believed. I'm not here to tell you to forget. I'm here to show you that you can heal without pretending the past didn't happen. Without the shame, guilt, or the blame.

These pages are a journey from silence to truth, from broken places to whole ones, from wounds you didn't choose to strength you *can*.

If you carry scars that still ache, I wrote this for you.

Chapter 1 — When Childhood Wasn't Safe

Scripture Reflections

"He will cover you with His feathers,
and under His wings you will find refuge."
— Psalm 91:4

"The Lord is close to the brokenhearted
and saves those who are crushed in spirit."
— Psalm 34:18

"Whoever welcomes one such child in my name
welcomes me."
— Matthew 18:5

These verses were chosen because:

- Your childhood wasn't safe, but God's protection never left you.
- Your heart was broken early, but God was close to you even then.
- You were not welcomed or cherished by the adults who should have protected you, but Jesus declares the worth of every child.
- Where humans failed you, God held you, protected you, and called you precious.

Loving Me

*I didn't hold much credence
in the notion of you having such
A strong affection for me.*

*The firm conviction of love
that you bestowed upon me
was hard to believe in its nature.
As many in the times, past,
have expressed such a state*

*of being dedicated
and loyal, yet their eventual
departure left me in anguish
and torment.*

*The one that was supposed to be
my female parent disposed
of me without a glance
back. If your own mother*

*doesn't think about you
with care or love,
how could I expect
anyone else to?*

*So, I passed through this
life perceiving everyone
would eventually embrace
this life without me.*

Then came one, I held great hope

*would remain. Little by little
I allowed my mind to believe,
to love, to take down the
encasement that held my heart
safe. I was finally loved...
or was I?*

*Although the time lingered
some, the warm fondness, or love
seemed to dissipate as it arrived...
little by little.*

*The encasement for my heart
began to build. But I found
it wasn't sufficient.
For when the time was ended,*

*the two-edge sword, that
was held, sliced
my heart over and over until
there were only small pieces
left behind.*

*How could I possibly
put it back together?*

*When I was just a broken
shell of myself lying
on the floor, He came,
He picked me up. He*

*said **I am yours and have always
been yours.** He told me He loved*

*me and has never stopped loving
me. He told me **If you draw near
to me, I will draw near to you.***

*He washed his love over me
and gave me a peace
that literally, is beyond
comprehension.
He told me, **I will never
leave you nor forsake you.***

*His love is like no other.
When I am lonely
I can cry out His name
and He calms the rage
that is inside of me.*

*He promised to provide
for the things that I need.*

*I now understand the notion
of affection He has for me
I now have the firm*

*conviction of the great
love that He bestows
on me. I no longer
worry about having someone
to love.*

*For He is always there…
loving me.*

When Childhood Wasn't Soft

Some people look back on childhood and see sunny afternoons, scraped knees, and the kind of safety that lets a kid believe the world is gentle. Children should be born into softness — into arms that are ready, into love that stays, into homes built to protect.
I wasn't one of those children. I don't have many memories like that.

My childhood was a place where I learned to read people's moods before I knew how to read books. I learned to be quiet before I ever learned to be confident. I learned that love could hurt, and that anger could arrive faster than I could make sense of it.

I wasn't given the luxury of innocence.
I was given lessons instead—painful ones.

Some memories come back softly, like they're walking on eggshells. Others come rushing in, heavy and sharp. I don't remember every detail, and honestly… I don't want to. Trauma does that—blurs the edges until only the impact is left. Thankfully. What I do remember is the way my small body learned to tense before a hand ever landed, the way I studied every expression, listening for danger in the tone of someone's voice.

That was safety to me back then: predicting the storm before it hit.

I grew up believing that being "good" might protect
me. That if I stayed quiet enough, helpful enough,
invisible enough, maybe I could avoid the next
blow. But abuse doesn't work that way. It doesn't
care how good you are. It doesn't care how much
you try to make yourself small. Pain still finds you.

And when you're a child, you don't have the words
to say,
This isn't okay.
This isn't normal.
I deserve better.

So instead, you say what children always say when
they have no other explanation:
"It must be my fault."

Those five words followed me into adulthood like a
dark shadow I never invited. They shaped the way I
loved, the way I reacted, the way I trusted, the way I
held myself together even when I was breaking.
Trauma has a way of teaching you lessons that
aren't true—but they feel true, because you learned
them before your brain was even finished growing.

I didn't understand why the smallest things could
make me jump or why sudden anger in a room felt
like a hurricane inside my chest. I didn't understand
why I apologized so quickly, even when I didn't do
anything wrong. I didn't understand why I kept
choosing people who took more from me than they
ever gave.

I only knew that the wounds were there… and that I
didn't choose a single one of them.

That kind of instability teaches you things you
shouldn't have to learn as a child:
how to sleep lightly, how to hide your emotions,
how to pretend nothing bothers you, how to adjust
quickly to survive.

I became skilled at reading rooms, reading faces,
reading moods — anything that might help me
avoid conflict or punishment. I learned to be overly
helpful, overly quiet, overly responsible. I believed
that if I could just be "good enough," maybe
someone would keep me.

But the truth is, children shouldn't have to earn
love.
They shouldn't have to perform for safety.
They shouldn't have to prove they're worth staying
for.

Yet that was the world I grew up in — a world
where love was uncertain and safety was temporary.

When you grow up in an environment where safety
is unpredictable, you start believing that everything
that happens is somehow your responsibility.
Children don't understand the failures of the adults
around them — they only understand their own
small world and their place in it.

So I learned to think:

If I were better, they wouldn't leave.
If I were quieter, they wouldn't get angry.
If I were easier to love, maybe someone would stay.

But let me say this clearly, for both of us:

A child should never have to earn safety. A child should never have to guess whether today will hurt. A child should never be blamed for surviving.

And yet, those of us who lived through it spend years trying to untangle the lies we absorbed along the way.

As I look back now, with the clarity and compassion I wish I had then, I see a girl who was doing her best with a world that failed her. I see a child who deserved protection, gentleness, guidance, patience—and who received fear instead.

My story began with a mother who was still a child herself. She was seventeen when she had me and only fifteen when she had my brother. She was trying to survive her own life, and the weight of motherhood was more than she could carry.

When she separated from my father, she faced a choice no mother should ever have to make:
go with her new boyfriend… or stay and raise her children.

She chose to leave.

She signed away her parental rights and walked out of our lives without looking back. She said she didn't feel anything for us.
People say you don't remember being abandoned — but your heart remembers. A part of me learned early that love could disappear in an instant.

My brother and I were placed into foster care, not together but split apart — like two pieces of a story being lived in different houses. The system tried to place us, move us, settle us… but nothing ever felt like home.

There were times when the foster system placed us briefly back with my father. But "home" was never safe with him. He and his third wife created an environment ruled by fear, not love.

Discipline in that house wasn't about teaching — it was about control.
We were made to sit against the wall as if we were sitting in an invisible chair, sometimes for prolonged periods. Our legs would shake, but stopping wasn't an option. Other times we were made to kneel on hard surfaces that caused pain, or we were placed in a cold, dark basement for hours — sometimes longer — with nothing to eat or drink.

Physical punishment was unpredictable. Whatever was close by could become part of it.

It wasn't about what we did wrong… it was about who held the power.

There were chores designed not to teach responsibility but to humiliate — like being forced to crawl on our hands and knees to pick tiny pieces of lint from the carpet. It was a way of breaking a child's spirit, piece by piece.

Growing up in that environment meant learning to sense danger before it arrived.
Listening for footsteps.
Watching faces.
Trying to make myself small, quiet, unnoticeable.
Trying to survive.

Woven through all of this was another kind of harm — one no child has the words to explain.

Before I was even old enough to understand what was happening, someone crossed boundaries that should never be crossed with a child. That violation continued until I was around 8 years old. I was told to keep quiet.

I didn't understand it.
I only understood the fear.
The confusion. The Pain.

The feeling that something was wrong but having no power to stop it. Was this how love was supposed to be? Was this him showing love? I didn't know, but what I did know is I didn't want any part of it. Unfortunately, I didn't have that luxury to choose.

Children don't have the language for violation. They only have instincts for survival. And for me, survival meant silence — holding it all inside because I didn't know there was another option.

When you grow up with that kind of fear and secrecy, it changes the way you see yourself. Children often take responsibility for things they could never have controlled. I carried that weight for years without knowing how deeply it shaped me.

By the time I was placed permanently into foster care, I was already holding more pain than most adults ever will. I entered the system as a two-year-old child who had learned too much about fear and not enough about love.

Growing Up in a System Instead of a Home

I stayed in the foster care system until I was fourteen.
Those years were a mix of constant change — new houses, new rules, new people, new expectations. Some places were gentler than others, but none of them felt like mine. I was always the child coming in with a trash bag of belongings, always the one trying to figure out how to fit into someone else's home.

The hardest part wasn't just the moving. But always leaving something behind, not by choice. The kids were cruel in the new schools; I was an outcast. I was ugly, I was unlovable. That's how I felt.

It was the feeling of not belonging anywhere. Not being allowed to fit in.

No one chose me.
No one claimed me.
No one stayed.

Yet that was the world I grew up in — a world where love was uncertain and safety was temporary.

Those thoughts followed me into adulthood like a dark shadow I didn't know how to shake. They shaped the way I loved, the way I reacted, the way I feared losing people. Even years later, the smallest shift in someone's tone or expression could make my heart race in ways I couldn't explain. I didn't know then that my body was reacting to years of learned danger.

This chapter isn't just about where I came from. It's about where so many of us come from. Pain doesn't make you weak. Survival doesn't make you dramatic. Having wounds you didn't choose doesn't make you broken, it makes you human.

The truth is, trauma teaches lessons long before a child can understand them.

It teaches them to survive — but it also teaches
them to blame themselves.

Looking back now, with the clarity and compassion
I didn't have then, I know this:

I wasn't the problem.
I wasn't the cause.
I wasn't the reason for the hurt that happened in
those home.

But as a child, I couldn't see that. I couldn't believe
any other way.
Children rarely can.

And so, the wounds I didn't choose became part of
the way I learned to move through the world —
always watching, always bracing, always trying to
be "good enough" for someone to keep.

Today, when I look back at that little girl — the one
who lived through abandonment, chaos, fear, and
things no child should ever endure — I see her
differently.

I see her strength.
I see her courage.
I see the way she kept going, even when every part
of her world said she shouldn't have to.

She survived what should have broken her.
She held onto hope without knowing she was doing
it.

She became the foundation of the woman I am now
— the woman writing these words.

This chapter isn't just about my past.
It's about every person who grew up with wounds
they never asked for.

If your childhood wasn't safe…
if your memories carry more fear than warmth…
if you learned to survive instead of play…
I want you to hear this clearly:

You survived something you never chose.
You endured pain you never deserved.
And you are allowed — fully, completely allowed
— to heal.

This is where our journey begins.
Not in shame.
Not in silence.
Not in pretending "it wasn't that bad."

It begins in **truth**.
In naming what hurt us, so we can finally lay down
what was never ours to carry.

The **truth** of knowing God chooses us, loves us,
laid down his life for us.

And with every step forward, we remember this:

We were never alone.
Not then.

Not now.
Not ever.

And yet, those of us who lived through it spend years trying to untangle the lies we absorbed along the way. We run, not knowing we are searching for something to fill the hole in our heart. Until we finally realize, we don't need to run anymore.

As I look back now, with the clarity and compassion I wish I had then, I see a girl who was doing her best with a world that failed her. I see a child who deserved protection, gentleness, guidance, patience—and who received fear instead.

If your childhood wasn't safe, if your story starts with wounds instead of warmth, I want you to know something:

You weren't responsible for the harm.
You didn't invite it.
You didn't deserve it.
And you're allowed to heal from it.

This is where our journey begins—telling the truth about what hurt us, so we can finally lay down what was never ours to carry.

Chapter 2 — The Lies Trauma Teaches Us

Scripture Reflections

*"The light shines in the darkness,
and the darkness has not overcome it."*
— John 1:5

*"You are precious in My sight, honored, and I love
you."*
— Isaiah 43:4

*"You will know the truth,
and the truth will set you free."*
— John 8:32

These verses were chosen because:

- Trauma taught you lies in the dark, but God's light has always been stronger.
- You were treated as if you weren't enough, but God calls you precious and honored.
- You carried shame that wasn't yours, but God's truth frees you from every lie.
- The emotional shadows of your childhood cannot stand against the truth of who God says you are.

Lessons Learned in the Dark

Trauma doesn't just wound the body or the heart.
It teaches.

Quietly, deeply, and over many years, it teaches us
things about ourselves and the world — things that
are not true but feel true because we learned them in
the dark.

When you grow up in chaos, fear becomes familiar.
When you grow up with rejection, you begin to
expect it.
When you grow up unseen, you start to believe
you're invisible.

Nothing wounds a child more deeply than the lies
whispered into their spirit by the people who should
have protected them. Lies like:

"You're not wanted."
"You're not worth staying for."
"You're the problem."
"You're too much."
"You don't matter."
"You are Ugly"

A child doesn't know these are lies — they become
the air she breathes. They shape the way she walks
into rooms, the way she loves, the way she
apologizes, the way she waits for the next
disappointment.

I didn't just survive trauma.
I learned from it — but not in ways that helped me.
I learned to expect pain.
I learned to minimize myself.
I learned to blame myself for the choices of others.
I learned to believe I wasn't enough.

But here is the truth I couldn't see then:

Darkness teaches lies.
God speaks truth.

God never once said I was unwanted.
God never once said I wasn't enough.
God never once said I deserved the hurt that
happened to me.

Those ideas came from broken people — not from a
perfect God.

We are told in Psalm 139:14 *"I will praise thee; for
I am fearfully and wonderfully made"*

For a long time, I didn't understand how deeply
those early lies had rooted themselves in me.
I didn't realize that the fear of being left wasn't
about the present — it was an echo from the past.
I didn't realize that apologizing for everything
wasn't politeness — it was survival.

I didn't realize that feeling "not enough" had
nothing to do with my worth — it was something I
was taught by people who never saw my value.

When Pain Becomes Identity

Trauma has a way of slipping into adulthood disguised as personality:

We call it **overthinking**, but it's really hypervigilance learned in childhood.

We call it being too sensitive, but it's really the emotional bruises that never got a chance to heal.

We call it **neediness,** but it's really the longing for affection we never received.

We call it **avoiding conflict**, but it's really the memory of how conflict used to explode.

We call it **staying quiet**, but it's really fear of being punished for speaking.

But the most damaging lie trauma teaches is this one:

"It was your fault."

That lie settles into the bones of a child who cannot make sense of cruelty or abandonment. It shapes the way she sees every relationship, every disappointment, every moment where she feels "too much" or "not enough."

I believed that lie for years.
Until God began telling me something different.

God's Whisper in the Shadows

He began showing me:

- That my worth was never tied to the people who walked away.
- That my identity was never defined by the pain I survived.
- That I was loved long before anyone failed me.
- That what happened to me was not who I was.
-

God's truth didn't erase the past — but it began to **reclaim** me from the lies that past had planted.

The hardest part about growing up with trauma is that the lies don't feel like lies.
They feel like *truth* because they were learned so early, whispered so quietly, and repeated so often.

But God has a way of shining light into places that have been dark for too long.
Not all at once — He knows that would overwhelm us.
But little by little, truth begins to push back the shadows.

For me, it started with small moments.
Moments where I felt seen.
Moments where I realized I wasn't the problem.
Moments where I sensed a love that didn't depend on performance or perfection.

God didn't shout His truth at me.
He whispered it —

the same way the lies had once been whispered,
but with gentleness instead of fear.

He whispered:

"You are Mine."
"I have always been with you."
"What they said about you is not who you are."
"You are precious to Me."

Imperfectly Perfect

You have known me since the eternal days
When the darkness hid not from you
When the night shined like the day
In your book you had already placed me
Where I was written, yet there was none of me
Then you placed me in my mother's womb
I was brought forth into the world in which you
fashioned
Where no occurrence happened without reason.

I knew you not.

When pain reached down into my soul when I was
young

Your hands held me and led me

When I started drinking to escape my past

You compassed my path

When I was beaten by a man that I loved

You were there. I was not hidden from you

When I fell to the lowest, darkest parts of me

You saw me, my substance, me, imperfect

Unhappy and ashamed with this life I'd been living
Feeling unworthy in this life I was given
Everything that I touched soon fell apart
Lost and alone with no love in my heart

So I took that handful of pills not wanting to wake.

The next morning you made me rise, with tears in
my eyes.
I couldn't go on, for this life was too long. My heart
with unrest,
I failed every test. I called out to you, what can I
do? I fell down
On my knees, begging you please, come unto me, I
have nothing
Left, my life is a mess. Only you in my life will do...,
Oh Lord, would you?

You came to me when you were weak and afraid

*As you traveled down your path, I carried you most
of the way.
I knew each time what you would do and what you
would say
And I loved you anyway.
Did you really think I'd leave you and turn my love
away?*

*I am here to stay. For you, I will never reject
For I know that you are imperfectly perfect.*

Shedding the Shame That Never Belonged to Me

And slowly, I began to understand:

**The darkness that shaped me could not define
me.
The lies that wounded me could not claim me.
God's truth was stronger than everything I had
been taught to believe.**

That realization didn't take the pain away instantly.
Healing isn't sudden.
It's a slow unlearning, a steady replacing of the old
with the new —
light pushing out darkness, truth replacing lies,
identity being restored piece by piece.

And God, patient as always, walks with us through
every step.
As God's truth began to take root in me, I started to
recognize just how many of my thoughts, reactions,

and fears had been shaped by what I survived — not
by who I really was.

I wasn't "too emotional."
I had learned to feel deeply because no one ever
helped me carry the weight.

I wasn't "too clingy."
I had learned to hold on tightly because people had
always let go.

I wasn't "hard to love."
I had simply never been loved in healthy ways.

I wasn't "broken."
I was healing from a childhood that fractured pieces
of me before I even knew who I was.

This is the truth trauma survivors often miss:

**What you learned in the dark is not your
identity.**

Your reactions were not flaws — they were
adaptations.
Your fears were not weakness — they were
protection.
Your tears were not dramatic — they were evidence
that your heart survived what was meant to crush it.

Relearning Who I Really Am

God doesn't look at us and see the coping
mechanisms we developed to survive.
He sees the child who deserved gentleness.
He sees the heart that kept trying.
He sees the strength that carried us through years of
what others may never understand.

And He says:

"You are Mine."
"You are loved."
"You are chosen."
"You are not defined by what happened to you."

The more His truth spoke into my life, the more I
realized something important:

**Trauma may have written the first chapters of
my story,
but God gets the final say.**

The lies trauma teaches are heavy.
Some of them settle so deeply that we mistake them
for our own thoughts.
But every time God speaks truth over us, something
shifts.
Something loosens.
Something healing begins.

There comes a moment in every survivor's journey
where you start to realize:

"Maybe the darkness wasn't telling me the truth."

Maybe you were never unwanted.
Maybe you were never the problem.
Maybe you were never "too much."
Maybe you were never meant to live small or quiet
or afraid.

Maybe — just maybe — the world lied about who
you were long before you had the chance to
discover who God says you are.

And who does He say you are?

Loved.
Chosen.
Held.
Seen.
Valued.
Protected.
Redeemed.
His.

God's truth doesn't argue with the lies of trauma; it
replaces them.

Light doesn't wrestle with darkness; it simply
shines and darkness disappears.

That is what healing looks like —
not forgetting,
not pretending,

but allowing God's truth to be louder than your past.
Slowly, gently, and in His timing, He guides us out
of the shadows and into a new understanding of
ourselves:

We are not what happened to us.
We are who God created us to be.

And the lies that once shaped us begin to fall away,
replaced with something stronger, steadier, and far
more beautiful:

Identity.
Worth.
Truth.
Light.

The kind only God can give.
The kind no one can take away.

God's truth doesn't argue with the lies of trauma; it
replaces them.
Light doesn't wrestle with darkness — it simply
shines, and darkness disappears.
Slowly, gently, and in His timing, God guides us out
of the shadows and into a new understanding:

We are not what happened to us.

We are who God created us to be.

And what He says about us is the only truth that
stands.

Chapter Three — Loving People Who Leave

Scripture Reflections

"I will never leave you nor forsake you."
— Hebrews 13:5

"When my father and my mother forsake me,
then the Lord will take me up."
— Psalm 27:10

"I have called you by name;
you are Mine."
— Isaiah 43:1

These verses were chosen because:

- humans left you, but God never did.
- your parents abandoned you, but God claimed you.
- your relationships failed, but God stayed.
- every earthly rejection was met with His promise:

"You are Mine."

When Leaving Becomes a Pattern

Some wounds bleed long after the moment they're
made.
Abandonment is one of them.
When you grow up with people who walk away,
you start to believe that love is temporary… that
staying is optional… that you have to earn every bit
of affection you get.

My understanding of love was shaped long before I
had my first relationship.

My mother left before I was old enough to speak.
My father was present only in body, not in safety.
Foster homes changed like seasons.
The only person who truly saw me — my brother
— wasn't allowed to stay with me.

Love, to me, was something that *disappeared.*

So, when I became a teenager — hurting, desperate
for safety, longing for connection — I didn't fall
into relationships.
I **ran** into them.

Not because I was reckless.
But because I was searching for what I never had:

Someone who wouldn't leave
Someone who wouldn't hurt me
Someone who would choose me
Someone who would stay

But when your first lessons in love are built on pain, betrayal, and instability, you end up searching for comfort in places that feel familiar… even if familiar wasn't safe.

That's how the cycle begins.

The Hope That Someone Has Changed

When I was fourteen, I wanted one thing more than anything else:

to be wanted.

So, when my father started visiting me at the foster home I was living, telling me that things were different now… that his wife had changed… that it would be better this time…
I wanted so badly to believe him.

Children — even when they're almost grown —
will always hope a parent has finally learned how to love them.

So, I packed up what little I had and went back.

But it wasn't better.
The same fear, the same cruelty, the same instability that marked my childhood were still there. The promises were empty. The change was imagined.
The hope I carried in my chest shattered faster than I could understand.

And once again, I had to learn the hardest lesson a child can learn:

Some people don't become safe just because we need them to be.

Leaving again wasn't rebellion.
It was survival.

So, I ran away from home — not to be reckless, not to cause trouble — but because staying meant drowning in the same pain I had been raised in.

The Mother I Longed For

Somewhere inside me, there was still hope that someone, somewhere, would choose me. So when I reconnected with my biological mother, I went to her — desperate for a relationship that might finally feel like love.

She lived in California, and I traveled across the country with the hope of a daughter in her chest.

But the home I walked into wasn't full of love.
It was full of resentment, anger, and coldness.
It felt like I represented a mistake she wanted to forget.
She didn't see me… she only saw her regrets.

And the girl who had already been abandoned once was abandoned again — not with paperwork this time, but with harshness, rejection, and emotional cruelty.

She wanted to send me back to Maine to live in another foster home.
I wasn't going back.
Not again.
Not after everything I had survived.

I left.

Not because I didn't want a mother.
But because she didn't want a daughter.

Into the Arms of Someone Much Older

At not quite fifteen, with nowhere safe to land and no one choosing me, I ended up moving in with a man seven years older than me. Not because I understood relationships, but because I understood survival.

He wasn't safety.
He wasn't protection.
He wasn't love.

He became another chapter of hurt — and another place I had to gather my strength and walk away.

I spent several years running, searching, searching for someone to love me.

Chasing the Kind of Love I Never Received

When you've been abandoned by the people who
were supposed to love you first,
your heart learns to chase love in places that feel
familiar —
even if familiar wasn't safe.

As I grew older, I stepped into relationships not
with confidence, but with hope… and with wounds
that kept choosing the wrong people.

Another Wound I Never Asked For

There is a kind of pain that freezes a moment in
time —
not because you remember every detail,
but because your heart remembers the shock, the
confusion,
and the feeling of being powerless.

When I was eighteen, someone I knew — someone
I trusted enough to let into my life — crossed a
boundary that should never be crossed. I was raped
by someone I cared about. Someone I called friend.

I didn't understand why it happened.
I didn't understand what I did wrong.
I didn't even have the words for it back then.

But I know now:

It wasn't my fault.
It wasn't my shame.
It wasn't my burden to carry.

And yet, for years, the emotional weight of it settled
into the same place as all my other wounds — the
place that whispered:

"This is why you're not worth loving."
"This is why people leave."
"This is why everything falls apart."

Trauma has a cruel way of stacking itself on top of
trauma,
layer after layer, until pain becomes the language
you understand best.

But even then —
even in that darkness —
God was there,
quiet but present,
holding the pieces I didn't know how to carry.

The Bond That Kept Me Going

Through all of this, there was one constant in my
life —
my brother.

Even though we didn't grow up together,
we were connected in a way that defied explanation.
It wasn't unhealthy or strange.
It was the kind of closeness you sometimes see in

twins —
two souls who shared the same beginning,
the same wounds,
the same deep understanding of each other's pain.

He was the one person I didn't have to explain
myself to.
He didn't need my story — he lived the other half
of it.

When he became paralyzed from the waist down
after his accident,
I went back to Maine to be close to him.
Not out of obligation,
but out of something deeper —
that bond we carried since childhood,
that sense that we were two halves of the same
survival.

Losing him later on didn't just break my heart.
It took a piece of me with him.
He was the mirror of my childhood,
the proof that I wasn't crazy,
the reminder that I hadn't imagined the pain.

And when he died,
I had to learn how to stand alone again —
but this time, without the one person who always
understood. The only one that loved me
unconditionally and stayed in my life. This was one
of the hardest losses I have ever dealt with.

I continue to carry that extreme loss, not just of my brother, but the unconditional love from him I never got from anyone else as I was growing up. I could always count on him being there.

Learning Love Through Loss

Every relationship I stepped into after that carried the weight of my past:

- I feared abandonment because I had been abandoned.
- I tolerated cruelty because cruelty felt familiar.
- I mistook attention for love because I had never known about healthy affection.
- I stayed too long because I didn't believe I deserved better.

But all of this wasn't because I was weak.
It was because I was wounded.
And wounded people don't look for perfect love —
they look for familiar survival.

It would take years before I would learn the difference
between someone who uses your wounds
and someone who helps you heal them.

The First Real Relationship — Betrayal Instead of Comfort

I married a man who seemed different — calm,
decent, stable.
I wanted a family, a child, something that felt like
home.
But he didn't want the same life.
And instead of leaving honestly, he left in pieces —
in secrets, in lies, in other women.

The final betrayal was the deepest:
he cheated with a young girl who had a baby —
a picture-perfect family that wasn't mine.
It wasn't the affair alone that hurt.
It was the feeling that once again,

someone had chosen someone else over me.

The wound wasn't just heartbreak.
It was abandonment all over again.

Once again, I am alone.
To start all over… again.

**The Marriage with Good Intentions, but Hidden
Battles**

The next man I was with wasn't cruel.
He wasn't violent.
But he carried battles of his own —
and his addiction to gambling fractured everything
we tried to build.

I kept trying to fix things.
I kept trying to make it work.

But you can't build a steady home on unstable
decisions.

Eventually, we separated —
not because I didn't care,
but because caring wasn't enough to change him.

**The Next Relationship — A Repeat of Old
Wounds**

Then came a man who brought back the fear I tried
so hard to escape.
He was extremely abusive.
He cheated on me as well.

It was the same cage I had lived in as a child,
just in a different house,
with a different face,
but the same pattern.

And once more…
I had to get away from him…this time it was harder.
Because I felt that I deserved it. I didn't.

Will anyone love me and not hurt me? I didn't
believe it, so I put up with the abuse for a while.
Until I couldn't.

Not because I wanted to start over —
but because I wanted to stay alive. I felt he would
eventually kill me; I had to survive.

A Marriage That Lasted Nearly Twenty Years

And then there was the man I stayed with for almost
two decades —
a long marriage that looked stable from the outside,
but was built on emotional exhaustion on the inside.
He was a narcissist.
Everything had to be about him —
his needs, his feelings, his choices.

If I wanted to do something for me, it caused him
great anger because I didn't have that time for him.

I didn't realize for years how deeply I was
disappearing inside that marriage.
Then, suddenly — without warning — he filed for
divorce.
Two weeks before he walked out, he had already
opened a separate bank account, already hired an
attorney, already planned the exit, already prepared
for a life without me. I had no clue.

And he cheated, too.

It wasn't just the betrayal.
It was the shock —
the realization that someone could live beside me
for years
and still be planning to leave behind my back.
Planning to hurt me for no good reason. I hadn't
done anything to deserve the pain he inflicted on
me. He tried to devastate me financially, physically,

and emotionally. Yet he was the one that left. He made me feel small, unloved, used, and unworthy.

The devastation of that pain nearly broke me. For three years I suffered emotionally at what he did. What he tried to do and wondered, did he really ever love me or was I just a tool. One that he could command, order, take advantage of and then throw away.

By the fourth year, I had been listening to Christian music often and praying a lot. I decided that I wasn't going to just survive anymore. I was going to live. I was going to keep my head up and make my life better. I wasn't just going to survive anymore. I wanted to thrive.

And for the first time in decades…
I finally stood alone and stayed alone, not just as a survivor, but as a person in control of my own destiny.

No longer waiting,
not searching,
but healing.
Healing for me.

But it wasn't easy. I fought every day.

God gave us two feet so we can take one step at a time.
Sometimes just one minute at a time. I stepped out and took control of my life.

Standing Alone for the First Time

After my 20 year-long marriage ended, I didn't run
into another relationship.
I didn't go searching for someone to fill the
emptiness.
I didn't chase love the way I used to.

For the first time in my life…
I stopped.

I stood alone —
not because I wanted to,
but because I **needed** to.

I needed to breathe without fear.
I needed to stop apologizing for existing.
I needed to hear my own thoughts without someone
else's anger drowning them out.
I needed to learn who I was when no one was
demanding that I shrink, hide, or endure.

Those four years were painful,
but they were holy too. I drew closer to God, I
relied on Him to heal me, to love me, to show me
the way.

That was the season where God began showing me:

what love was
what love wasn't
what I had survived
what I deserved

and what healing actually felt like

It wasn't loud.
It wasn't sudden.
It wasn't dramatic.
It was slow.
Gentle.
Quiet.

Like light slipping under a door in a dark room.

For the first time, I wasn't trying to be enough for
someone else.
I was learning to be enough for myself —
and to believe that God saw me as enough even
when I didn't.

How God Rewrote My Understanding of Love

During those years, God didn't just comfort me.
He began to **re-educate** my heart.

He showed me:

- that love isn't supposed to hurt.
- that someone staying isn't a gift you have to
  earn.
- that "being chosen" isn't supposed to feel
  like a miracle — it's supposed to feel
  normal.
- that safety isn't a privilege — it's a right.
- that real love speaks softly, not loudly.

- that love doesn't shout, threaten, disappear, or betray.

For the first time, I began to understand a truth I had spent my whole life living without:

Love doesn't leave.
People do —
but love, real love, the kind that God teaches —
stays.

When you learn that truth, really learn it,
the world looks different.
Relationships look different.
You look different.

And it prepared me —
quietly, carefully —
for someone who would show me what love was
meant to be all along.

When Safe Love Finally Arrived

After everything I had survived — every
abandonment, every betrayal, every wound —
I never expected to meet someone who would love
me in a way that felt safe. I didn't go looking for it.

But healing has a way of preparing your heart for
things you once believed were impossible. God
brought love to me when I least expected it. I still
wasn't sure I wanted it, nor did I believe I was
ready, but here it was before me.

When my current husband came into my life, I
didn't fall fast.
I didn't fall blindly.
I didn't fall because I was lonely.
I connected with him because something in me felt
at peace around him —

a feeling I had never experienced before. He made
me laugh, he made me feel like I was the only one
in the room, he made me nervous because of my
wounds. Would he love me still if he knows? Would
he stay when I have a bad day? I was scared of
opening the door again….

He didn't raise his voice.
He didn't make me shrink.
He didn't make me afraid to speak or breathe or be
myself.
He didn't demand perfection.
He didn't punish vulnerability.

He simply saw me —
not the broken pieces,
not the past,
not the wounds —
me.

And that was new.
Beautiful.
Terrifying.

Because when you've spent your life with people who leave,
you expect the leaving even when someone stays.

There were moments when he traveled,
and old fears tried to convince me he was doing
something wrong,
that he would vanish like everyone else had,
that I wasn't enough to be chosen by someone good.

But he always came home.
He always reassured me.
He always listened, held me, laughed with me, and
stayed.

He stayed.

He stayed when I struggled.
He stayed when my fears surfaced.
He stayed when my past tried to sabotage my
present.

One day he said something that marked me:

**"One of the reasons I married you is because of
your stubbornness to love me."**

After everything I had been through,
he saw my love not as a flaw,
not as desperation,
but as a *strength*.
Something beautiful.

Something worth choosing.
Something worth committing to.

That is what love is supposed to feel like —
not fear,
not confusion,
not uncertainty,
but safety.
Not perfection,
but presence.

Not performance,
but partnership.

He didn't replace my need for God —
he simply became one of the ways God healed my
understanding of love.

Every relationship I had before him was shaped by
my past:
the fear of being left,
the belief that I wasn't enough,
the pattern of choosing people who mirrored my
childhood pain.

But this relationship taught me something different:

Love doesn't abandon.
Love doesn't injure.
Love stays.

And when safe love finally entered my life,
I realized something I had never fully believed:

**The problem was never that I wasn't lovable.
The problem was that I had never been loved
right**.

Real love doesn't fix all wounds —
but it reminds you that you weren't meant to carry
them alone.
I still have those wounds, but God is helping me
heal through my husband.

Helping me know that I am beautiful and loveable.

Chapter 4 — The Quiet Weight of Self-Blame

Scripture Reflections

"Come to Me, all you who are weary and burdened, and I will give you rest."
— Matthew 11:28

"There is therefore now no condemnation for those who are in Christ Jesus."
— Romans 8:1

"He heals the brokenhearted and binds up their wounds."
— Psalm 147:3

These verses were chosen because:

- You carried shame that was never yours to hold.
- You blamed yourself for things done to you, not by you.
- God offers rest where guilt once lived
- He replaces condemnation with compassion.
- His healing speaks louder than your history.

The Lies That Sound Like Your Own Voice

Some weights don't come from the outside.
They grow inside you — quietly, slowly, piece by

piece — until you're carrying guilt you never earned.

For survivors, self-blame becomes its own language:

"I should have known better."
"I should have stopped it."
"I'm so stupid."
"It must have been something I did."
"Maybe I deserved it."
"If I were enough, they wouldn't have left."

These thoughts settle so deeply that they start sounding like truth.

But they're not truth.
They're the echoes of trauma — the lies planted when you were too young to fight them.

You weren't taught love.
You were taught responsibility for things that were never yours:

- The cruelty of adults
- The choices of others
- The abuse you endured
- The abandonment you lived through
- The violence that surrounded you
- The betrayal you suffered as an adult
- The rejection that repeated itself in your relationships

Children can't make sense of cruelty, so they take
the blame for it.

That's what I did.
Not because I was weak —
but because I was trying to survive in a world that
refused to protect me.

And those old beliefs didn't disappear when I
became an adult.
They grew with me.
They followed me.
They shaped my relationships.
They shaped the way I loved.
They shaped the way I feared.

They shaped the way I saw myself.

But here's the truth God whispers into that old
shame:

"None of this was your fault."
Not then.
Not later.
Not ever.

Where the Blame Comes From

Self-blame doesn't grow in a vacuum.
It grows in the spaces where love should have lived
and didn't.
It grows in the silence where comfort should have
been.

It grows in the confusion children feel when adults behave in ways that make no sense.

When you were hurt as a child, you didn't think:

"Something is wrong with them."

No child thinks that.

Instead, you thought:

"What did I do wrong?"
"Why am I not enough?"
"Why won't they stay?"
"Why isn't love safe for me?"

And because the pain kept repeating —
abandonment, cruelty, instability, betrayal —
the belief repeated too.

Every time someone walked away…
Every time someone hurt you or blamed you…
Every time you tried your best and still weren't chosen…
Every time love felt like punishment…

The same lie got heavier:
"It must be me."

But that wasn't truth.
That was trauma —

teaching you responsibility for the actions of broken people.

You were a child in impossible circumstances.
You survived things that would have crushed most adults.

You coped with what you had, with what you understood,
with the little emotional tools you were given.

You didn't choose the pain.
You only learned how to live through it.

But here's the hardest part:

**When trauma becomes familiar,
guilt becomes instinct.**

It follows you into adulthood,
into relationships,
into heartbreak,
into silence,
into the moments where you wonder if the problem is still you.

But it's not.
It never was.
And God has been trying to hand you the truth piece by piece:

"This weight never belonged to you."

When God Begins to Lift the Shame

Shame is heavy, but it's also sneaky.
It settles quietly into the places trauma once lived,
and it whispers things you would never say to
another person:

"You should have stopped it."
"You should have known better."
"You let it happen."
"You weren't worth staying for."
*"If my own mother doesn't love me, why should I
expect someone else to?"*

These thoughts feel like your own voice…
but they are not your voice.
They are the echo of someone else's choices,
someone else's actions,
someone else's sin.

And God has never agreed with a single one of
those lies.

God doesn't speak in shame.
He speaks in truth.
He speaks in identity.
He speaks in love.

His voice sounds more like this:

"Come to Me, you who are weary... I will give you rest."
(Matthew 11:28)

"There is no condemnation for you."
(Romans 8:1)

"I heal the brokenhearted... you included."
(Psalm 147:3)

God does not blame you for what you lived through.
He mourns it.
He stands with you in it.
He carries what you cannot.
He lifts what you were never meant to hold.

And in the quiet moments —
the moments when the world slows just enough for
Him to speak —
He begins to untangle the shame from your soul.

Not with force.
Not with demands.
Not with pressure.

But with gentleness —
the kind of gentleness you were never given as a
child.

He whispers truth into the places where lies once
lived.

He reminds you:

"You were a child. It was not your fault."
"You were abandoned, but I never abandoned you."
"You were hurt, but I saw you, and I stayed."
"You were made to feel unworthy, but I call you
Mine."

Every time He speaks truth, a little piece of shame
loosens.

This is how healing begins —
quietly, softly, slowly —
like dawn breaking through a night that lasted far
too long.

How Self-Blame Followed Me into Adulthood

Even long after the hurt stops,
the beliefs you learned in the dark keep echoing.

The child who once thought,
"It must be my fault,"

grows into an adult who still apologizes for things
she didn't cause.

The child who thought,
"If I were better, they would stay,"
becomes a woman who works twice as hard in
relationships that don't deserve her effort.

The child who thought,
"I should have stopped it,"

becomes an adult who carries the weight of guilt
she never earned.

You didn't enter adulthood as a blank slate.
You carried every lie trauma taught you:

- You blamed yourself when relationships began to crumble
- You blamed yourself when someone cheated
- You blamed yourself for choosing people who hurt you
- You blamed yourself for "not seeing it coming"
- You blamed yourself for staying too long
- You blamed yourself for not being enough
- You blamed yourself when people left, even when they were the ones wrong

Self-blame became a familiar companion —
not because you deserved it,
but because it was the only explanation you were
ever taught.

When marriages failed, you wondered:

"What's wrong with me?"

Not:

"What's wrong with someone who betrays, lies,
cheats, or hurts?"

When partners mistreated you, you thought:

"I must not be lovable."

Not:

"Some people cannot love because they are broken themselves."

When relationships ended, you assumed:

"I wasn't enough."

Not:

"They were never capable of staying."

These lies followed you from childhood into adulthood
because they had never been challenged.

No one had taught you differently.

But God had been waiting —
waiting to break those patterns

with truth,
with love,
with presence,
with healing.

And every time someone left,
every time someone betrayed you,
every time someone hurt you…
God remained.

He didn't walk away.
He didn't change His mind.
He didn't blame you.
He didn't tire of you.
He didn't abandon you.

And every moment of pain —
every abandonment, every betrayal, every
heartbreak —
became one more place where God whispered:

**"This was never your fault.
And it never will be."**

Laying Down What Was Never Yours to Carry

There comes a moment in every survivor's story
when the weight becomes too heavy to keep holding
— a moment when you realize the guilt you've
carried your entire life never belonged to you in the
first place.

It belonged to the ones who abandoned you.
It belonged to the ones who hurt you.
It belonged to the ones who lied, betrayed,
manipulated, or mistreated you.
It belonged to the adults who failed you when you
were a child.
It belonged to the people who chose cruelty over
kindness.
It belonged to the broken hearts of others — not
yours.

You carried the shame of other people's sins.
You carried the blame for other people's choices.
You carried the weight of hurt you never deserved.
You carried the silence of things you were too
young to understand.

But God has been whispering something different
over you:

"Give it to Me."

Not because you have to earn forgiveness.
Not because He blames you.
But because He knows you were never meant to
carry this weight.

God doesn't hand shame to His children —
He removes it.
He doesn't point out your failures —
He heals your wounds.
He doesn't condemn you —
He covers you in grace.

And slowly, you begin to see how deeply He has
been working:

- You survived what tried to break you
- You endured what should have crushed you
- You carried more than anyone should ever
  carry
- And you are still here

Not because you were perfect,
but because you were **beloved**.

When God rewrites your story,
self-blame loses its voice.
Shame loses its power.
Fear loses its grip.

You begin to understand the truth:

"I am not what happened to me."
"I am not the choices of those who hurt me."
"I am not responsible for the sins of others."
"I am free."

And that is the freedom trauma tried to steal —
the freedom God returns into your hands
with gentleness, patience, and love.

This is how healing begins:

not in guilt,
not in fear,
not in shame —
but in surrender.

You are releasing the burden you were never meant
to carry.
You are stepping into the truth of who God says you
are.
You are standing in light, no longer shaped by the
dark shadows.

And God is whispering over you, with more love than you've ever known:

**"You were never to blame.
Not for any of it."**

CHAPTER FIVE — Rebuilding the Pieces of Me

Scripture Reflections

*"Those who wait on the Lord shall renew their strength;
they shall mount up with wings like eagles."*
— Isaiah 40:31

"Be still and know that I am God."
— Psalm 46:10

"In quietness and trust shall be your strength."
— Isaiah 30:15

These verses were chosen because:

- You spent years rebuilding your life in quiet places.
- You found your strength again — not quickly, but slowly, in God's timing.
- Healing came to you in stillness, not chaos
- God met you in solitude and renewed what pain had drained.
- Your strength didn't come from people… it came from Him.

These verses reflect the holy work God did when you finally had room to breathe

When Everything Falls Quiet

There are seasons in life when God pulls you out of the noise —

not to punish you,
not to isolate you,
but to heal you in ways the world is too loud to allow.

After years of heartbreak, abandonment, betrayal, and survival, I entered into a season that felt unfamiliar:

Silence.
Stillness.
Aloneness.

But this time, I was not alone because someone left me.

I was alone because God was clearing space for the rebuilding.

For the first time in my life:

I wasn't walking on eggshells
I wasn't trying to fix someone
I wasn't apologizing for existing
I wasn't fighting to be enough

I was surviving… I was breathing

It wasn't an empty silence — it was a sacred one.
A silence where God began whispering truths I had
never been able to hear over the noise of other
people's brokenness.

A silence where the weight I carried for years
finally began to loosen.

A silence where God began to give me something I
had never been allowed to hold:

Myself.

This was the beginning of rebuilding — not the
rebuilding of a home or a marriage or a life with
someone else…
but the rebuilding of *me*.

The pieces pain had scattered were finally being
gathered into something whole — slowly, gently, in
God's hands.

The Work God Did in the Quiet

Solitude has a way of revealing things noise keeps
hidden.
When life finally slowed down,
when no one else's anger filled the rooms,
when no one was demanding pieces of you,
when the heartbreak finally settled into stillness —

God began working in places that had never been touched before.

Not all healing happens in church pews.
Sometimes it happens:

- in the quiet hours of the morning
- in the silence of your living room
- in the moments when your mind finally stops running
- in the tears you cry without anyone watching
- in whispered prayers when you don't know what to say
- in the breath you didn't realize you'd been holding for years

This is where God met you.

And instead of asking you to be strong…
He became your strength.

Instead of asking you to hold everything together…
He held you.

Instead of asking you to understand the past…
He began rewriting the way you saw it.

In the quiet, God began healing things you thought were permanent:

the fear of being left
the shame you'd carried since childhood

the pain of old relationships
the guilt that wasn't yours
the belief that you were unlovable
the exhaustion of constantly surviving

He peeled back the layers gently —
never forcing, never rushing, never overwhelming.

And piece by piece, in the kind of stillness you had
never been allowed in childhood,
God began showing you who you were underneath
the trauma:

Not the abandoned girl.
Not the broken woman.
Not the one who wasn't enough.
Not the one people walked away from.

Someone beloved.
Someone chosen.
Someone worth rebuilding.

Little by little, the quiet became a sanctuary —
a place where you weren't defined by who left,
but by the God who stayed.

He was there when I cried myself to sleep.
He was there when I didn't want to get out of bed.
He was there when all I could do was speak His
name.

Finding the Strength I Didn't Know I Had

For most of my life, strength looked like survival:

- staying quiet
- enduring pain
- navigating chaos
- trying to be enough
- carrying burdens alone
- building a life without a foundation
- loving people who didn't love you back
- rising every time you were knocked down

But in this season of solitude,
strength began to look different.

It wasn't frantic.
It wasn't fearful.
It wasn't desperate.
It wasn't the strength of a woman bracing for
impact.

It was a quiet strength —
the kind that grows when God rebuilds you from the
inside out.

It sounded like:

- saying "no" for the first time
- choosing peace over chaos
- letting go of people who drained you
- no longer chasing those who left

- recognizing red flags you once ignored
- trusting your instincts
- speaking up instead of shrinking
- believing you were worth something better

It looked like:

- waking up without dread
- feeling your lungs expand with real breath
- laughing without fear of consequence
- enjoying silence instead of fearing it
- caring for your body, your mind, your heart
- rebuilding your life one small piece at a time

Strength became less about holding everything together
and more about letting God hold you. Walking in the faith that God has got this.

And slowly, I began to see a version of myself
that trauma had covered for years:

A woman who is brave.
A woman who is tender-hearted and resilient.
A woman who survived what should have destroyed her.
A woman who still chooses love, despite everything she's endured.
A woman who God has never once let go of.

Healing didn't happen all at once.
But every day, I felt something shifting —
a steadiness, a clarity, a quiet power.

And for the first time in my life,
I was starting to recognize my own worth,
my own voice,
my own identity —
not shaped by pain,
but shaped by God.

This was the beginning of becoming whole.

Preparing My Heart for Something New

Those four years alone weren't wasted time.
They were the years God used to prepare my heart
for a kind of love I had never known,
a kind of peace I had never felt,
a kind of life I didn't believe I could have.

In the past, I entered relationships from a place of
survival —
searching for safety, validation, belonging,
connection.
But in this season, something shifted:

I wasn't searching anymore.
I wasn't desperate for someone to choose me.
I wasn't trying to fill the emptiness inside.
I wasn't trying to fix someone else to prove my
worth.

I was learning to choose myself
in a way I had never been taught.
And when I finally stood on my own two feet —
not out of heartbreak,

not out of fear,
but out of healing —
my heart was ready for something different.
Something healthy.
Something steady.
Something safe.

It wasn't about being perfect.
It wasn't about being confident every day.
It wasn't about suddenly forgetting my past.

It was about stepping into love
without losing myself this time.
About being open
without being blind.
About trusting
without ignoring the truth.
About loving
without carrying all the weight alone.

The years by myself taught me:

- how to recognize red flags
- how to listen to my intuition
- how to set boundaries
- how to be honest with myself
- how to walk away from anything that hurts my soul
- how to take care of my emotional health
- how to let God guide my steps instead of my wounds guiding me.

These years weren't punishment.
They were preparation.

God wasn't keeping love from me—
He was strengthening me so I would finally be able
to receive love
without losing myself in the process.

He was preparing me
for the man who would come next —
not to replace my pain,
but to walk with me through my healing.

A love that didn't demand silence,
that didn't punish vulnerability,
that didn't abandon me,
that didn't break me.

A love that felt like peace.
A love I didn't have to earn.
A love God had been preparing my heart to
recognize.

Becoming Whole Again

Rebuilding isn't just about putting the broken pieces
back together.
Sometimes it's about discovering that **some pieces
were never meant to stay,**
and that God is creating something new in their
place.

By the time my years of solitude came to an end,
I wasn't the same woman who had entered them.
The woman who walked into that season was
exhausted,
carrying pain she thought would follow her forever.
She was still shaped by trauma,
still battered by heartbreak,
still unsure of her worth.

But the woman who walked out?

She was different.

She carried strength in her bones —
not the strength of survival,
but the strength of healing.

She had clarity —
the ability to see truth without fear clouding her
vision.

She had boundaries —
not walls to keep people out,
but gates that protected her peace.

She had a voice —
one she no longer silenced to make others
comfortable.

She had self-respect —
the quiet kind that grows when you finally
understand your worth.

And she had something she had never truly had
before:

**A sense of self not shaped by pain but shaped by
God.**

Healing didn't erase my past —
it redefined my future.

I began to realize:

I are not the abandoned girl
I are not the woman others misused
I are not the mistakes I made
I are not the shame I carried
I am not the fears that once controlled me

I am someone redeemed.
Someone restored.
Someone strengthened by God's own hands.
Someone worth loving in the right way.

My solitude wasn't a season of emptiness —
it was a season of becoming.

God didn't rebuild me into who I used to be.
He rebuilt me into who I was always meant to
become.

And with a stronger heart, clearer eyes, and a
steadier spirit,
I was finally ready for the chapter that comes next
—

a chapter where love doesn't break you...
but blesses you.

CHAPTER SIX — A Love That Didn't Break Me

Scripture Reflections

"Behold, I am doing a new thing;
now it springs forth—do you not perceive it?"
— Isaiah 43:19

"There is no fear in love;
but perfect love casts out fear."
— 1 John 4:18

"The steadfast love of the Lord never ceases;
His mercies never come to an end."
— Lamentations 3:22

These verses were chosen because:

- This chapter is the beginning of a new kind of love — one God brought into your life in His perfect timing.
- You learned that real love doesn't create fear, it removes it.
- God was faithful through every heartbreak, and He was faithful in leading you to someone who would love you the right way.
- These verses show how God heals, restores, and replaces fear with peace.

- They declare that your story didn't end in pain — God created something new and beautiful out of what tried to break you.

Learning to Trust with a Heart That Had Been Hurt

Even when love is safe,
fear doesn't disappear overnight.

A wounded heart doesn't suddenly forget
everything it survived.

It remembers:

the people who left
the promises broken
the nights filled with fear
the betrayals that came without warning
the pain that arrived disguised as love

So when I began this new relationship,
the fear whispered familiar lies:

"He's going to leave."
"Something is wrong."
"You're too much."
"You're not enough."
"You can't trust this."

Not because he did anything wrong —
but because my past had taught me that good things never stayed.

But he stayed.

When fear made me quiet, he didn't pull away.
When I asked questions shaped by old wounds, he
didn't get angry.
When I hesitated or doubted myself, he gave
reassurance instead of resentment.
When I expressed my fears, he listened instead of
judging.
When I struggled to believe I was lovable, he
showed me patience I wasn't used to receiving.

Little by little, day by day,
he became a safe place for my heart to rest —
something I had never known before.

And with every moment he stayed,
the fear lost some of its power.

This was God's healing at work —

not loud,
not dramatic,
but steady.

God used his consistency to heal my fears.
He used his gentleness to soften old wounds.
He used his presence to remind me that love isn't
supposed to hurt.

For the first time,
I wasn't loving from desperation or survival —
I was loving from healing.

And that kind of love changes you.

It teaches you:

- that you are worth staying for
- that you deserve peace
- that love doesn't have to be earned
- that affection shouldn't come with fear
- that trust isn't weakness, it's courage
- that God can bring someone into your life
  who honors the heart others broke

This was the beginning of real trust —
not the blind kind,
not the desperate kind,
but the steady, healthy, God-guided kind
that grows only after you've learned who you are.

When Fear Spoke… and Love Spoke Louder

Even in a healthy relationship,
fear doesn't just vanish.
It shows up quietly,
in small moments,
in old instincts that surface without warning.

Fear showed up when he traveled.
Not because he gave me reason to worry,
but because the past had taught me

that whenever someone left,
they usually didn't come back the same.
Fear showed up in silence.
Not because silence meant danger,
but because in my past,
silence was always the moment before pain.

Fear showed up when I was happy.
Not because joy wasn't real,
but because I had learned that happiness
was often followed by heartbreak.

Fear showed up when I loved him deeply.
Not because my love was wrong,
but because I had loved people deeply before
and still ended up hurt.

Fear didn't come from him.
It came from the memories of everyone who had
failed me.

But love — real love — met those fears one by one.

When fear told me,
"He's probably doing something wrong,"
he answered with transparency and reassurance.

When fear whispered,
"This is too good to last,"
his consistency proved otherwise.

When fear said,
"You're too much,"

he showed me I was enough —
not by words alone,
but by how he treated me.

When fear tried to convince me
that love was dangerous,
his gentleness reminded me
that love was meant to be safe.

And with every moment he stayed,
with every honest conversation,
with every quiet demonstration of loyalty,
a little more fear melted away.

This wasn't just about trusting him.
It was about trusting God's faithfulness.

God didn't bring him into my life
to repeat the heartbreak of my past.
He brought him to **heal** parts of me
that had been hurt for far too long.

Healing doesn't happen all at once.
It happens in small moments —
moments where love proves that fear
doesn't get the final say.

And those small moments
began forming a truth in my heart
that trauma had tried to erase:

Safe love exists.
And I am worthy of it.

The Moment I Realized This Love Was Different

There wasn't one dramatic moment
where everything suddenly became clear.

No movie-scene revelation.
No overwhelming declaration.

It was quieter than that.
Gentler.
Almost unnoticeable at first.

It was in the way my body stopped bracing when he
walked into the room.
In the way my heart stopped racing whenever he
left for a trip.
In the way my thoughts softened instead of
spiraling.
In the way I no longer felt the need to apologize for
every emotion.

It was in the peace.

A peace I had never felt in any relationship before.
A peace that didn't come from perfection,
but from presence.
From partnership.
From honesty.
From a man who understood me,
and chose to love me with steadiness,
not chaos.

I realized this love was different
when my fears stopped being louder than his
actions.

He proved—over and over—
that love is not something you chase…
it is something you receive.

He showed me:

- consistency without control
- affection without manipulation
- commitment without conditions
- honesty without cruelty
- patience without frustration
- love without fear

And slowly, something inside me shifted.

I wasn't waiting for him to leave.
I wasn't expecting betrayal.
I wasn't searching for signs of danger.
I wasn't losing myself to please him.

I was **safe**.

And that safety didn't come from him alone —
it came from God's faithfulness working through
him.

God had spent years preparing my heart
to recognize a love that wasn't shaped by trauma
but shaped by Him.

A love that didn't break me.
A love that didn't silence me.
A love that didn't ask me to disappear.
A love that didn't punish me for being human.

A love that felt like healing.

And one day, quietly,
I realized something I never thought I'd believe:

"This is what love is supposed to feel like."

How Safe Love Helped Rewrite My Story

Being loved safely didn't erase my past,
but it changed the way I carried it.

It softened memories that once felt sharp.
It quieted fears that once felt overwhelming.
It reminded me that the world wasn't only full of
people who hurt,
but also people who stay.

For the first time in my life:
I wasn't walking on eggshells.
I wasn't trying to interpret anger.
I wasn't bracing for betrayal.
I wasn't shrinking to make myself acceptable.
I wasn't apologizing for existing.
I wasn't trying to earn love like it was a privilege.

Instead, I was learning what it meant to:

- breathe without fear
- love without losing myself
- rest without suspicion
- speak without trembling
- exist without guilt
- trust without carrying the weight alone

This kind of love didn't "fix" me —
God had already begun that work long before.

But it *supported* the healing.
It *protected* the healing.
It *honored* the healing.

And in that environment of safety and truth,
something beautiful happened:

I became more myself
than I had ever been before.

He didn't complete me —
God did that.
But he complemented the woman God was shaping
me into.

He didn't replace the strength I gained in solitude
—
he respected it.
He didn't silence my past —
he understood it.
He didn't erase the wounds —
he helped me carry them.

This was the first time love wasn't another battle, but a blessing.

The first-time intimacy wasn't tied to fear.
The first-time commitment wasn't tied to control.
The first-time affection wasn't tied to manipulation.
The first-time loyalty wasn't tied to lies.

This wasn't luck.
This wasn't coincidence.
This wasn't just *"finding the right person."*

This was **God's** faithfulness.

A promise kept after years of prayers whispered in the dark.
A restoration of everything pain tried to take.
A reminder that God doesn't break His children —
He heals them.
He strengthens them.
And yes…
He sends people who love them the way He intended all along.

This chapter of my life doesn't end with "happily ever after."
It ends with something better:

Restored.
Redeemed.
Loved without fear.
Held by God's faithfulness.

And for the first time,
love didn't take from me —
it gave.

Chapter Seven — God Never Left Me

Scripture Reflections

*"Even when I walk through the darkest valley,
I will fear no evil,
for You are with me."*
— Psalm 23:4

"I will never leave you nor forsake you."
— Hebrews 13:5

*"The Lord your God goes with you;
He will never leave you nor abandon you."*
— Deuteronomy 31:6

These verses were chosen because:

- They reflect the truth of your entire life:
  even in the darkest places, God was there
- Human love failed you, but God's love
  remained constant
- Every abandonment was met with His
  presence
- Every moment of fear was met with His
  comfort
- This chapter is the testimony of His
  faithfulness from childhood until now

Looking Back Through New Eyes

There were years in my life when I wondered why
everything hurt so much, and all the time,
why the people who were supposed to love me
didn't stay,
why safety felt impossible,
why heartbreak seemed to follow me like a shadow.
Why, while others always seemed happy, I always
had to have it hard.

But now, looking back through the eyes of healing,
I can say something I didn't always believe:

God never left me.
Not once.
Not for a moment.
Not in the darkest places of my childhood.
Not in the confusion of my teenage years.
Not in the heartbreaks of adulthood.
Not in the silence.
Not in the storms.

He was there when no one else was.
He was holding things together when I felt like
everything was falling apart.
He was strengthening me when I didn't have the
strength to move.
He was whispering truth when lies tried to drown
out everything good.

There were moments when I thought I was alone,
but now I see that those were the moments
God was carrying me the most:

When I survived things no child should experience
When I ran from places that were hurting me
When I cried into pillows so no one would hear
When I begged for love that didn't come
When people I trusted betrayed me
When I held shame that wasn't mine
When I stood at the edge of giving up
When I found myself on my knees, asking God
what to do with my life

In all of it —
every tear, every fear, every heartbreak, every quiet
moment —
God was present.

I didn't always feel Him.
But His presence doesn't depend on my feelings.
His faithfulness isn't fragile.
His love doesn't leave.

And throughout my life,
He had one message written over every chapter in
my life:

"I am here."

That truth changed everything.

Why I Still Believe

I've had people look at my life —
at the trauma,
the abandonment,
the abuse,
the heartbreak,
the losses —
and ask me with genuine confusion:

**"How can you still believe in God after
everything you went through?"**

My answer is simple:

How could I not…

**Because without God,
I never would have made it through**.

Faith wasn't the result of an easy life.
It was the anchor that held me in a life that was
anything *but* easy.

People see the scars and wonder how I could still
trust God.
But what they don't understand is this:

**God wasn't the one who hurt me.
People did.
People with free will, brokenness, and their own
unhealed wounds.**

God wasn't the cause of the pain —
He was the comfort in it.

He didn't abandon me —
He was the one who stayed.

When adults failed me,
when family walked away,
when relationships shattered,
when I cried alone at night,
when I blamed myself for things that weren't my
fault,
when I was drowning in shame,
when I didn't want to keep living…

**God was the only presence that remained
constant.**

I didn't believe in God because my life was good.
I believed in God because my life was hard —
and I survived anyway.

I believed because:

- In the moments when I should have broken,
  I didn't.
- In the moments when I should have died, I
  lived.
- In the moments when I had no strength,
  something carried me.
- In the moments when I had no hope, a
  whisper inside me said, "Hold on."

- In the moments when I fell apart, grace held the pieces together.
- In the moments when I was afraid, He gave me peace.

People see the suffering and ask how I can believe in God.

But I look at everything I survived,
everything I walked through,
every moment I almost gave up yet, somehow kept going,
and I ask:

How could I not?

Pain didn't destroy my faith.
Pain *revealed* my faith —
because it revealed the One who never left me in it.

The Protection I Didn't Recognize Until Later

Looking back now,
I can see God's fingerprints all over moments
that once felt like abandonment.

When I was younger,
I mistook survival for luck
and protection for coincidence.
But now I understand something deeper:

God was protecting me even when I didn't know I needed protecting.

He protected me in ways that were invisible at the
time:

**By giving me the strength to endure what no
child should endure**

— strength no one taught me, strength I didn't ask
for,
but strength that kept me alive.

**By placing people in my life for a season who
gave me just enough hope to keep going**

— a teacher, a foster parent, a stranger who spoke
kindness,
moments that softened the blow of a harsh world.

By pushing me out of dangerous situations

even when it felt like rejection,
even when I didn't understand why the doors were
closing.

By letting certain relationships end

— not to punish me,
but to save me.

**By giving me a heart that still believed in
goodness**

even after being treated with cruelty.

By whispering strength into me in the darkest moments

— the nights I cried alone,
the moments I felt worthless,
the times I didn't want to keep living.

By guiding my steps even when my path made no sense

— because He knew where I was headed
long before I did.

By keeping my heart soft

when trauma tried to harden it.

By making me leave places that would have destroyed me

even when I was afraid of the unknown.

Sometimes God's protection looks like miracles.
Sometimes it looks like strength.
Sometimes it looks like survival.

And sometimes it looks like heartbreak —
because heartbreak removed me from people
who were never meant to hold my future.

I didn't understand it then.
But now I see that every step,
every tear,

every closed door,
every painful ending
was leading me toward something better —
toward healing,
toward peace,
toward the life I have now.

God wasn't silent.
He was shielding me.
He wasn't absent.
He was leading me.

And despite everything I went through,
one truth became clear:

I was never alone.

Where God Spoke into My Healing

There is a moment in healing
when pain begins to make sense
—not because the hurt was good,
not because it was deserved,
but because God starts revealing
how He has been weaving purpose
through every broken piece.

I spent years asking God *"Why?"*
Why the abandonment.
Why the abuse.
Why the heartbreak.
Why the loneliness.

Why I had to carry so much so young.
Why my life looked so different from others.'

But slowly, as healing unfolded,
the questions changed.

**Instead of asking, "Why did this happen to me?"
I began asking, "How can God use this through
me?"**

God didn't give me the pain,
but He refused to let the pain define me.

He took what was meant to break me
and turned it into:

strength
wisdom
compassion
discernment
resilience
empathy
and a testimony that has already touched more lives
than I realize

The very experiences that once filled me with
shame
became the ones God used to open doors for healing
— for myself,
and now for others.

When I prayed through tears—
begging God to show me why my story was so
heavy—
He spoke to my heart in the quietest way:

**"Because one day, your story will help someone
else survive theirs."**

And that truth changed everything.

My brokenness wasn't wasted.
My survival wasn't meaningless.
My tears were not forgotten.
My scars became evidence of God's mercy,
not evidence of His absence.

He showed me:

- that I can offer hope to those who feel
  hopeless
- that I can speak life into those who feel
  unworthy
- that I can understand pain others can't put
  into words
- that I can love deeply because I know what
  lovelessness feels like
- that I can comfort others because God
  comforted me

This is the redeeming power of God—
not erasing the past,
but transforming it.

Every part of my story
that once felt like a wound
became part of my purpose.

God turned what hurt me
into what now helps me guide others.

He turned my survival
into testimony.

He turned my tears
into wisdom.

He turned my loneliness
into compassion.

And He turned every piece of my hurt
into a chapter that leads others toward Him.

My Life Is Proof That God Never Left Me

Who am I?

Years later, another truth surfaced—one I never expected. DNA testing revealed that the man I believed was my biological father wasn't, and the sister I thought was mine by blood wasn't either.

My whole life of whom I was changed in an instant. I was no longer who I thought I was, I didn't belong where I thought I did. I was devastated, blown away, aghast, but really there were no words to describe how awful I felt with the revelation of this.

I wanted answers and the man I thought was my father had already passed away. My sister had already passed away. I guess that was God's grace that I didn't have to tell them. I had already lost them once.

When I confronted my biological mother, she refused to admit anything. She denied ever having an affair. She insisted that she would never have done that to my father. It stunned me. It felt like the ground shifted again, another piece of my identity shaken loose. And the man who was my biological father didn't even know I existed—lost in a long line of children he never cared for.

For a moment, it felt like another abandonment, another unanswered question. But then God whispered to my heart: *"Your identity was never built on them. It was built on Me."* And in that truth, I found peace. My life is proof that even when humans fail you, deny you, or forget you, lie to you—God never does. He knew who I was all along.

Looking back over the years—
over the broken pieces of my childhood,
over the wounds left by people who should have protected me,
over the heartbreaks and losses,
over the nights I cried into my pillow,
over the moments when I didn't know how I would keep going—
I see one truth woven through every memory:

God never left me.

Not when I was abandoned.
Not when I was afraid.
Not when I was hurt.
Not when I was unloved by people who should have
loved me.
Not when I blamed myself for what others did.
Not when I was lost in trauma.
Not when I made mistakes trying to fill the
emptiness inside.
Not when I thought my life had no purpose.
Not even when I didn't want to live.

He was there.

In the strength I didn't know I had.
In the moments I survived without understanding
why.
In the peace that came out of nowhere when I
needed it most.
In the whispers that told me to hold on.
In the doors He closed to protect me.
In the people He removed for my safety.
In the love He sent at the right time.
In the healing that flowed through years of silence.
In the light that broke through the darkest nights.
In the hope that never fully went out—
even when I thought it had.

God was not the author of my pain.
But He became the healer of my wounds.
The protector of my heart.

The restorer of my soul.
The strength in my weakness.
The comfort in my loneliness.
The One who held me when no one else did.

My life is not a story of what people did to me.
My life is a story of what God carried me through.

And if I stand here today—
whole, healed, loved, purposeful—
it is not because I am strong on my own,
but because God was faithful
in every moment I couldn't see His hand.

This is my testimony:

People left.
God stayed.
People broke me.
God rebuilt me.
People failed me.
God never did.

And that is why I believe.
That is why I have faith.
That is why I can speak hope into this world.
Because the same God who never left me
will never leave you either.

This is the truth that anchors my entire story:

God has been with me every step.
And He *always* will be.

So now, how do "you" heal?

PART ONE: Stepping Into Healing

Where Healing Truly Begins

Every healing journey begins with one truth:

God is for you.
He is with you.
He wants your healing even more than you do.

You are not walking into healing alone.
You are walking with the One who saw every hurt,
who knows every wound,
who understands every fear,
and who has been carrying you long before you
even realized it.

Healing feels overwhelming when you think you
have to do it by yourself.
But you don't.

You were never expected to.

God's heart toward you is not anger.
Not disappointment.
Not judgment.

His heart toward you is:

- compassion

- gentleness
- protection
- restoration
- patience
- deep, unwavering love

When you take your first step toward healing,
He is not standing at a distance waiting to see if you
get it right.

He is already beside you,
guiding you,
strengthening you,
holding you steady,
and whispering:

**"I am with you.
You're not doing this alone."**

God is not against you — He is for you.

He doesn't condemn you for the wounds you carry.
He doesn't shame you for the feelings you struggle
with.
He doesn't rush you, push you, or demand
perfection.

He heals gently.
He works slowly and kindly.
He restores what was broken in a way that doesn't
overwhelm your heart.

Healing is not something you achieve.
Healing is something God leads you through.

Your part is not to be strong —
your part is to be willing.

Willing to let Him in.
Willing to trust Him with the parts of you you've hidden.

Willing to let Him rewrite the places where pain once lived.

Because every step forward in healing begins with Him.

And He is on your side.

Healing begins at the moment you finally say:

"I don't want to carry this anymore."

Not when everything makes sense.
Not when the pain is gone.
Not when the past feels distant.
Not when you feel strong.

Healing starts the moment you choose to stop surviving
and allow God to begin restoring.

Most people think healing means:

- forgetting the past
- pretending it didn't happen
- forcing themselves to "be fine"

But real healing doesn't erase what happened.

Real healing changes what the pain means.

Healing begins when you:

- stop blaming yourself
- stop minimizing what hurt you
- stop ignoring the voice inside you
- stop expecting yourself to "just get over it"
- stop carrying responsibility that was never yours

And instead, you start:

- inviting God into the parts of you that still ache
- giving yourself permission to feel
- letting go of the shame that wasn't yours
- seeing your worth through God's eyes
- learning what safety and peace look like

Healing begins with honesty.
Not the kind that tears you down,
but the kind that frees you:

**"I was hurt.
I didn't deserve it.
And I want to heal."**

That's where the shift happens.

Because God will never force healing on you —
but the moment you open the door,
even a crack,
He steps into the room.

Your healing doesn't depend on perfection.
It depends on willingness.

The willingness to say:

"God, I'm ready."

Even if you're trembling when you say it.

Letting God into the Places You've Never Touched

For many survivors, letting God into the wounded
places is harder than it sounds.

Not because they don't believe in Him.
Not because they don't want healing.
But because those parts of the heart have been
locked away for years —
sometimes decades.

Those rooms feel dangerous,
painful,
overwhelming,
or even shameful.
But here's the truth you need to hold onto:

**God already knows what's inside those rooms.
And He's not afraid of any of it.**

He's not shocked by your memories.
He's not disgusted by your pain.
He's not surprised by your reactions.
He's not disappointed in your wounds.

He has seen every tear you cried in silence.
He was there in every moment you felt alone.
He understands your heart better than you do.

Letting God in isn't about revealing something He
doesn't know.
It's about letting Him comfort, heal, and restore
what He already saw.

So how do you let God in?

A Simple Invitation to Jesus

If you've never let Jesus into your heart,
I want you to know this:
it's never too late,
and it's not complicated.

God isn't asking you to be perfect.
He isn't asking you to have all the answers.
He isn't asking you to clean yourself up first.
He simply wants you—
as you are,
right now.

All you have to do is pray and tell Him:

**"Jesus, I believe You are the Son of God.
I believe You died for my sins and rose again.
I know I fall short, and I make mistakes,
but I want You to wash me clean.
Come into my heart.
Show me the way.
Be my Savior."**

And that's it.

In that moment,
your sins are wiped clean,
your past no longer defines you,
and you become a child of God.

A daughter of the King.

And here is the most beautiful truth:

**Once you belong to Him,
you can never lose your salvation.
Not because you're perfect,
but because He is.**

No mistake you make
can undo God's forgiveness.
No failure can remove His love.
No weakness can separate you from Him.

You are His—
now and forever.

A Necessary Part of Healing: Forgiveness

There is one more truth I need to share with you—
not because it's easy, it is definitely not easy,
but it's freeing:

We must forgive the ones who hurt us.
Not for them.
For us.

Forgiveness does **not** mean:

- what they did was okay
- you have to trust them again
- you have to reconcile
- you have to forget
- you have to give them access to your life
- you have to pretend the pain didn't happen

Nope, no way is that necessary.

Forgiveness simply means
you are choosing to release the hold their actions
still have on your heart.

It is letting God lift the bitterness,
the anger,
the resentment,
the emotional weight
that keeps you tied to something you no longer want
to carry.

Because the truth is:

**Unforgiveness keeps you connected to the pain.
Forgiveness connects you to freedom.**

I don't expect you to forgive and instantly feel
healed. Sometimes forgiveness is not a moment but
a journey. You may have to forgive that person
every day for a while.

Each time you do, you release a little more of the
pain and a little more of the control they once had
over your heart. With time, God replaces that
weight with peace.

Forgiveness is not a feeling.
It's a decision.

A quiet moment when you say:

**"God, I release this person into Your hands.
Heal the part of me that was wounded.
I'm letting go."**

It doesn't happen all at once.
Sometimes you forgive in layers,
as God heals deeper parts of your heart.

But every time you choose forgiveness,
you choose healing.
You choose peace.
You choose to take back your power.
You choose to move forward.

Forgiveness doesn't make you weak.
It means the wound *no longer controls your life.*

You are not saying,
"What they did was fine."
You are saying,
"What they did will not define me anymore."

And that is strength.
That is freedom.
That is God working through you.

Next are the simple steps that open the door to healing:

1. Start with honesty.

Not fancy prayers.
Not perfect words.

Just this:

**"God, this part of me still hurts.
I don't know what to do with it.
But I want to heal."**

Honesty is the key that unlocks the door.

2. Allow yourself to feel — without judgment.

God cannot heal what you refuse to acknowledge.

If something hurts, name it.
If something scares you, admit it.
If something feels heavy, don't minimize it.

God meets you in truth right where you are, not pretending.

3. Invite God into specific wounds.

Instead of saying, *"Heal me,"*
say:

- "Heal this fear."
- "Heal this memory."
- "Heal this place where I always blame myself."
- "Heal the part of me that still feels unlovable."

Specific prayers open specific places.

4. Let God comfort you before He changes anything.

Healing doesn't start with transformation.
It starts with comfort.

Sometimes the first thing God wants to tell you is:

"This wasn't your fault."
"You didn't deserve that."
"I was with you then, and I'm with you now."

Before He rebuilds,
He holds.

5. Be patient with yourself.

Letting God into deep wounds is a process, not a moment.
Some days you'll feel open.
Some days you'll feel guarded.

God is gentle with both.

He heals slowly enough that it won't break you,
and steadily enough that it will free you.

He won't leave you.

6. Remember: God does not force Himself in.

He knocks,
He invites,
He whispers…

But He waits for you to open the door —
because real healing requires willingness,
not pressure.

Your healing is safe with Him.

He loves you just the way you are.

Building Emotional Safety Within Yourself

Many survivors learned early in life that the world
was not safe.
That the people around them were unpredictable.
That emotions were dangerous.
That needs were "too much."
That the safest thing to do… was to stay small.
So healing requires learning something entirely
new:

How to feel safe inside yourself.

Not because life is perfect.
Not because everything is fixed.
But because emotional safety starts with the way
you treat your own heart.

Here's how to begin building that safety —
gently, steadily, and with God's help.

1. Speak to yourself the way God speaks to you

God never says:

"What's wrong with you?"
"You should be over this."
"You're too emotional."
"You're weak."

These voices come from trauma, not God.

God speaks with:

- compassion

- truth
- gentleness
- patience
- reassurance
- love

So ask yourself:

"Would God say this to me?"

If He wouldn't,
then you don't need to say it to yourself either.

This is the first step in creating emotional safety.

2. Give yourself permission to feel

Emotions are not a threat.
They are signals.

Fear says, "I was hurt before."
Anger says, "Something was unfair."
Sadness says, "I lost something important."
Numbness says, "This is too much right now."

Suppressing emotions doesn't make you strong —
it makes you disconnected.

Letting yourself feel is not weakness.
It is healing.

3. Create moments of peace on purpose

You don't have to wait for peace to find you.
You can create space for it intentionally.

Try:

- stepping outside for fresh air
- pausing to breathe deeply
- listening to worship music
- sitting somewhere quiet
- holding a warm drink
- praying a short, simple prayer
- placing your hand on your heart and saying, **"I'm safe now."**

Your nervous system learns safety through repetition.

4. Stop punishing yourself for trauma reactions

When your heart races,
when you shut down,
when you get scared,
when you react strongly —
you're not "crazy."
You're not "dramatic."
You're not "broken."

You are responding to things your body learned
from experiences that were too much.

Instead of judgment, try saying:

"This reaction makes sense based on what I lived through."

Compassion creates safety.
Judgment destroys it.

5. Let God be the source of your safety

You will feel safest when you anchor your heart to the One who never changes.

Invite Him into your emotions:

"God, help me feel safe with myself."
"Quiet my thoughts."
"Steady my heart."
"Remind me that I'm not alone."

God doesn't just protect your life —
He protects your inner world.

He makes your heart a place where healing can grow.

How to Stop Carrying What Was Never Yours

One of the deepest wounds trauma creates
is the belief that **everything is your responsibility:**

- other people's emotions
- other people's cruelty
- other people's abandonment
- other people's choices

- other people's sin
- other people's lies
- other people's brokenness

But here is the truth that sets you free:
You were never meant to carry what other people caused.

Letting go isn't forgetting.
Letting go isn't denying.
Letting go isn't minimizing the pain.

Letting go means **handing back the weight that was never yours in the first place.**

1. Identify what was never your responsibility

Some burdens feel like they belong to you
only because you carried them for so long.

But they are NOT yours.

You are *not responsible* for:

- the abuse you endured
- the adults who failed you
- the love you never received
- the betrayal you didn't deserve
- the people who left
- the lies you were told about yourself
- the harm done to you as a child
- the cheating, the manipulation, the rejection
- the anger or addictions of others

- the trauma responses you developed to survive

These were never your sins.
Never your faults.
Never your failures.

They were the failures of others.

2. Say the words: "This is not mine to carry."

You break trauma's power by naming what belongs to you
and what does **not.**

Try speaking these truths out loud or in prayer:

"Their choices are not my burden."
"Their sin is not my shame."
"Their cruelty is not my fault."
"Their leaving is not my identity."
"I release what was never mine."

Your heart needs to hear these words.
Your nervous system needs to hear them too.
And God stands with you as you say them.

3. Give the weight back to God

This is not something you do by pushing your emotions away.
You do it through surrender.

A simple prayer like:

**"God, I can't carry this anymore.
Take what was never meant for me."**

When you release the weight, you make room for:

- peace
- clarity
- healing
- truth
- rest
- self-compassion

And God is gentle —
He doesn't rip burdens out of your hands.
He takes them only when you're ready to let go.

4. Learn the difference between guilt and burden

Guilt is responsibility for *your* actions.
Burden is responsibility for *other people's* actions.

Healing requires separating the two
.

If you didn't cause the pain,
you don't carry the guilt.

If you didn't choose the harm,
you don't hold the responsibility.

5. Release people you tried to fix

Many survivors learned to "earn" love by fixing
broken people.
But that is not your purpose.

You can love people.
You can pray for them.
You can hope the best for them.

But their healing
is not your job.

They have to choose it, not you. You can't fix
someone that doesn't believe they need it.

And releasing that role
does not make you unkind —
it makes you free.

**6. Ask God to show you what truly belongs to
you**

When you feel overwhelmed or confused, pray:

**"Lord, show me what is mine,
and help me release what is not."**

He will show you gently,
piece by piece,
what was never meant for you to carry.

This is where healing grows.

Letting God Lead the Healing Instead of Fear

Healing is not just emotional work.
It's spiritual alignment.

Most survivors start healing from a place of fear:

- fear of repeating the past
- fear of being hurt again
- fear of trusting the wrong people
- fear of feeling broken
- fear of being too much
- fear of not being enough
- fear of failure
- fear of losing control

But fear cannot guide you into freedom.
Fear can only guide you back to survival mode.

To heal deeply, you must let **God** lead the journey
—

not fear, not shame, not insecurity, not old patterns.

Here's how to shift from fear-led healing
to God-led healing.

1. Name the fear — and hand it to God

Fear loses power as soon as you bring it into the
light.

Say:

**"God, I'm afraid of this.
Help me trust You more than I trust my fear."**

God doesn't expect you to be fearless.
He expects you to be honest.

Honesty opens the door.
God walks you through it.

2. Ask God, not fear, to interpret your emotions

Fear says:
"Something bad is coming."

God says:
"You are safe with Me."

Fear says:
"You're alone."

God says:
"I will never leave you nor forsake you."

Fear says:
"You can't trust anyone."

God says:
"I will guide you into truth."

Ask yourself:

**"Is this God speaking…
or is this my old trauma speaking?"**

One leads to freedom.
The other leads to fear.

3. Invite God to rewrite your reactions

Trauma taught your body to react fast —
to protect you when you were a child
and couldn't protect yourself.

But now you can pray:

**"God, heal the places where my reactions still
come from fear.
Teach my body that I am safe."**

Your nervous system responds to repetition.
God responds to willingness.

Together, they create healing.

4. Let God show you what is safe — not your memories

Fear always expects the past to repeat itself.
God does not.

He can show you:

- who is trustworthy
- what relationships are healthy

- when a boundary is needed
- when you're reacting to old hurt, not new harm
- when something is safe even if it feels unfamiliar

Healing happens when you let God guide your discernment
instead of relying on fear alone.

5. Trust God's timeline, not your impatience

Fear says, "Heal faster."
Fear says, "You're behind."
Fear says, "This should be done by now."

God says:

- "My timing is perfect."
- "You are not behind."
- "I am doing a work in you."
- "I heal gently."
- "I'm not rushing you."

You are not losing time —
you are gaining freedom.

6. Remember: God leads with peace, not pressure

Any voice inside you that sounds like:

- anxiety

- shame
- harsh criticism
- panic
- condemnation
- urgency

is **not** God.

God leads with:

peace
clarity
gentleness
patience
assurance
steady love

He never pushes.
He never shames.
He never overwhelms.

When God leads your healing,
you grow safely…
slowly…
steadily…

PART TWO: Healing With God

Learning to Recognize God's Presence in Your Healing

One of the most important parts of healing is realizing this:

**God is already in your healing —
you're not trying to bring Him into something
He hasn't begun.**

Most survivors expect healing to feel dramatic —
like a sudden breakthrough or a loud spiritual
moment.

But God usually heals in quieter ways that you
might miss if you aren't looking.

Healing with God often looks like:

- a moment of peace in the middle of anxiety
- a thought that lifts shame off your shoulders
- a Scripture that suddenly feels personal
- tears you didn't know you needed to cry
- strength you can't explain
- a memory that hurts a little less
- a sense of "I'm not alone right now"
- choosing a healthy boundary without guilt

- reacting differently to something that once overwhelmed you

These are not coincidences.
These are **God's fingerprints**.

How to recognize God in your healing

1. God's presence feels like peace, even if the situation hasn't changed.

Sometimes it's just a moment —
a breath
a calm thought
a feeling of being held.
That's Him.

2. God's voice never condemns.

If a thought sounds like:

"You're a failure"
"You should be over this"
"You're too much"
"You're weak"

That's not God.

God speaks with:

- compassion
- truth
- gentleness

- reassurance
- clarity
- love

3. God's presence brings clarity without confusion.

You may suddenly understand something about your pain.
You may see a memory differently.
You may feel permission to let go of something.

Clarity is God's way of healing the mind.

4. God's presence is patient.

He never rushes your healing.
He never pushes you past your capacity.
He works in layers —
the right wound at the right time.

If you feel rushed, that's not God.
If you feel gently led, that's Him.

5. God heals in moments that feel ordinary

A quiet morning.
A song.
A verse.
A conversation.
A moment of vulnerability.
A deep breath you didn't realize you were able to take.

Healing with God is not always dramatic.
It is often **steady, soft, and sacred.**

**Section 2 — How to Hear God's Voice Instead of
Shame**

One of the biggest challenges survivors face is this:

The voice of shame is loud.
The voice of God is gentle.

And if no one ever taught you the difference,
it's easy to mistake one for the other.

But God's voice and shame's voice
sound nothing alike.

Understanding this difference
is one of the most important steps in healing.

1. Shame's voice attacks. God's voice restores.

Shame says:

- "You're worthless."
- "You're the problem."
- "You should have known better."
- "Look what you did."
- "You're not good enough."
- "You're unlovable."

God says:

- "You are Mine."
- "You are forgiven."
- "You are loved."
- "You are chosen."
- "You are enough."
- "You are redeemed."
- "You are not defined by what happened to you."

If the voice tears you down, it is not God.

If the voice lifts you up, it is.

2. Shame is urgent. God is patient.

Shame pressures:

- "Fix it now."
- "Hurry."
- "Why aren't you better?"
- "You're behind."

God waits.

He does not rush.
He does not demand.
He does not threaten.
He does not overwhelm.

God leads you forward at a pace that honors your heart.

3. Shame confuses. God brings clarity.

Shame leaves you feeling:

- tangled
- uncertain
- lost
- overwhelmed
- guilty

God brings:

insight
wisdom
gentle understanding
truth that settles your heart

If a thought brings peace or a quiet "aha,"
that's God.

4. Shame makes you hide. God invites you closer.

Shame says:
"Don't pray about this. God is disappointed."

God says:
"Come to Me. I understand."

Shame pushes you away from God.
God draws you toward Himself with compassion.

5. Shame focuses on the past. God focuses on your future.

Shame drags up old failures.
God speaks vision and hope.

Shame says, "This is who you are."
God says, "This is who you're becoming."

God looks at you through what He is healing,
not through what you've survived.

6. Shame condemns. God convicts gently.

Condemnation tears you down.
Conviction builds you up.

Condemnation says:
"You are bad."

Conviction says:
"That wasn't right,
but I will help you grow."

Big difference.

7. How to start hearing God more clearly

You don't need perfect spiritual discipline.
Just willingness.

Here are ways to tune into Him:
Sit in silence for one minute and say,

"God, speak to me."

Open Scripture and ask,

"What do You want me to see today?"

Pause when you feel shame and say,

"Lord, show me the truth."

When fear rises, whisper,

"God, steady me."

Journal your feelings and then ask,

"God, what do You say about this?"

God's voice is already present —
healing is learning how to recognize it.

Rebuilding Trust in God After a Life of Pain

Trusting God doesn't always come naturally
when your life has been filled with trauma,
abandonment, or betrayal.

Many survivors love God
but struggle to trust Him.

Not because of who God is—
but because of what people have done.

This section is not about guilt.
It's about understanding yourself with compassion
so you can rebuild trust in a gentle, honest way.

1. It's normal to struggle trusting God when people have failed you

If those who were supposed to protect you didn't…
your heart learned a painful lesson:

"No one is safe."

Without realizing it,
you may project that belief onto God.

This is not rebellion.
It is a trauma response.

And God understands.

He is not offended by your fear.
He knows your heart
He is not impatient with your doubts.
He knows exactly why trusting feels difficult.

And He meets you there
with tenderness, not judgment.

2. Trust in God grows through consistency — not pressure

Trust doesn't grow because you force yourself to believe.
It grows because you experience God showing up.

Healing moments that build trust:

- a prayer answered in a small way
- a moment of peace when you needed it
- a burden suddenly feeling lighter
- a scripture speaking directly to your situation
- a fear loosening its grip
- clarity coming out of nowhere
- strength arriving when you felt weak

Trust grows through evidence, not effort.

3. God proves Himself through presence, not perfection of circumstances

Life may not have been easy.
But look at the places where you weren't destroyed—
that's God.

Look at the wounds that didn't kill you—
that's God.

Look at the strength that got you here—
that's God.

Look at the moments you didn't give up—
that's God.

He hasn't protected you from everything,
but He protected you through everything.

4. Rebuilding trust starts with small steps

You don't have to trust God with your whole heart
all at once.
Start small:

"God, help me with this moment."
"God, steady my anxiety."
"God, guide me today."
"God, show me what You see."

Trust is built brick by brick,
not by one giant leap.

**5. God never asks you for blind trust — only
honest trust**

Blind trust says, "I feel nothing, but I'll pretend."
Honest trust says, "I'm scared, but I'm trying."

God honors honesty more than performance.

**6. Your trust in God grows when you let Him
into your fear**

Fear is not the enemy of faith —
it's the doorway to deeper faith.

You can pray:

**"God, I want to trust You,
but this part of me is afraid.
Help my fear trust You too."**
This is a prayer God delights in.

Because trust doesn't grow in the absence of fear.
Trust grows when you invite God *into* your fear.

**7. Trust becomes easier when you realize God
has never left you**

When you connect the dots of your life—
the survival,
the protection,
the strength,
the doors that closed,
the doors that opened,
the healing that found you—

you begin to see:

God has been trustworthy all along.

And trust becomes less of a struggle
and more of a natural response.

**Experiencing God's Peace in Moments of
Anxiety**

Healing with God isn't only about big
breakthroughs.

It's also about the small, sacred moments where His
peace settles over your heart
when fear tries to take over.

Anxiety doesn't mean you lack faith.
It means your nervous system learned to stay on
high alert.

But God has peace that reaches deeper
than fear, memory, or emotion.

**1. Breathe slowly and invite God into the
moment**

When anxiety hits, the body panics before the mind
understands.

Start with this simple grounding prayer:

"God, be here with me right now."
"Steady my breath. Calm my heart."

Your breath signals your nervous system
that you are not in danger right now.

And when your breath softens,
your heart becomes able to sense God's presence.

2. Place your hand over your heart

This physical gesture communicates safety to your
body.

Then pray softly:

**"Lord, hold my heart.
Quiet the fear.
Fill me with Your peace."**

This shifts your focus from the fear inside you
to the God who surrounds you.

3. Speak Scripture that calms your spirit

You don't need long verses —
short, powerful ones settle the mind quickly:

"Peace, be still."
— Mark 4:39

"When I am afraid, I put my trust in You."
— Psalm 56:3

"Your rod and Your staff comfort me."
— Psalm 23:4

Let the truth steady you.

Let it anchor you.

4. Name the fear — then give it to God

Whisper:

"Lord, I'm afraid of ___."
"Take this fear from me."

Naming it pulls fear into the light
so God can lift it.

Silence is where fear grows.
Honesty is where fear breaks.

5. Remind yourself what is true right now

Anxiety is often rooted in memories or what-ifs.
God speaks into *this moment*.

Say:

"Right now, I am safe."
"Right now, God is with me."
"Right now, I am not alone."

Your nervous system responds to truth spoken out
loud.

6. Picture yourself in God's hands

Imagine:

- His arms around you
- His hand on your back
- His light surrounding you
- His presence covering your fear

Visualization is powerful for trauma survivors.
It gives your mind a safe place to rest.

7. Don't fight the anxiety — let God cover it

You don't have to force yourself to calm down.

You don't have to win a battle over your own
emotions.

You only need to lean into God so He can:

- quiet your mind
- settle your breath
- slow your heart
- relax your body
- speak peace into the moment

You're not calming yourself alone —
you're receiving peace from the One who never
leaves.

**Letting God Heal Your Memories
Without Reliving Them**

Many survivors fear healing because they think it
means
digging up every painful moment
or reliving every memory in detail.

But God does not heal that way.

He does not retraumatize you.
He does not drag you backward.

He does not make you re-experience the things that broke you.

He heals memories in a way that is:

- gentle
- slow
- safe
- and guided
-

You do not have to revisit the past to heal.
You only have to let God touch the places
where the pain still lives.

1. God heals the impact of the memory, not the memory itself

You don't need to remember everything.
You don't need to articulate every detail.
You don't need to explain anything to God.

He already knows.

What He heals is:

- the shame attached to the memory
- the fear connected to it
- the lies that formed because of it
- the emotional reaction it triggers
- the belief that it defines you

- the pain it still causes in the present

God doesn't need the memory replayed
to heal the wound it created.

**2. You don't have to open the whole story — just
the part that still hurts**

Sometimes all you can say is:

**"God, this still hurts…
please heal what I can't even put into words."**

That prayer is enough.

God can work with whispers.

3. Let God decide the pace of healing

You don't have to push yourself
or force yourself
or rush the process.

God heals in layers:

- when your heart is ready
- when your mind is steady
- when your body feels safe
- when the old wound won't break you to look
  at

If you're not ready to face something,
God will not make you.

4. When memories surface, they're not punishments — they're invitations

Sometimes a memory will resurface suddenly.
This doesn't mean you're going backward.
It means God is gently showing you:

"You're strong enough to heal this now."

It's not a setback.
It's a step forward.

5. God can rewrite the meaning of a memory without changing the memory

He can take:

- terror
- confusion
- loneliness
- shame
- helplessness

And rewrite it with:

- strength
- clarity
- truth
- dignity
- His presence

Your story stays the same,
but the *meaning* changes.

And that changes everything.

6. You can give God the memory without reliving it

Try praying this:

**"God, I give You this place inside me
that still hurts.
Heal it in the way only You can."**

Or:

"Lord, rewrite this memory with Your truth."

Or:

**"God, take the sting out of this memory
and replace it with peace."**

You don't have to relive the past.
You only have to surrender it.

7. Healing a memory is God giving you freedom, not more pain

When God heals a memory:

- the fear lessens
- the emotional reaction softens
- the shame breaks
- the lie loses power
- the pain fades

- your heart feels lighter
- your body relaxes
- you feel safe again

It is nothing like reliving the trauma.
It is relief.

It is freedom.

It is restoration.

It is God doing what only He can do.

PART THREE: Rebuilding Your Life

Learning Safe Love After Trauma

When your heart has survived betrayal, abuse,
neglect, or abandonment,
love becomes one of the hardest things to trust
again.

Not because you don't want love—
but because your heart learned to protect itself from
it.

You may long for connection
and fear it at the same time.
You may crave closeness
but freeze when it arrives.
You may desire healthy love
but be drawn to familiar pain.

This is not your fault.
It is what trauma does.

But the beautiful truth is this:

**You can learn love again —
the safe kind God always intended for you.**

1. Safe love is calm, not chaotic

Survivors often confuse chaos with passion
because chaos is what they grew up with.

Safe love feels different:

- steady
- slow
- warm
- predictable
- kind
- patient

It won't overwhelm your nervous system.
It won't make you question your worth.
It won't make you earn affection.

Safe love feels like peace, not adrenaline.

2. Safe love never makes you smaller

Unhealthy love requires you to shrink:

- your voice
- your needs
- your emotions
- your boundaries
- your dreams
- your worth

Safe love welcomes all parts of you.

It says:

"You don't have to disappear to be loved here."

3. Safe love respects boundaries

If someone becomes angry, guilt-filled, or distant because you set a boundary,

that is not safe love.

Safe love:

- listens
- honors your needs
- communicates without manipulation
- takes responsibility
- doesn't punish you for protecting your heart

Boundaries don't scare healthy people away.
Boundaries expose unhealthy people.

4. Safe love is consistent

Unhealthy love swings between:

- affection and withdrawal
- kindness and cruelty
- promises and disappointments
- warmth and coldness

This keeps your nervous system in a constant state of confusion.

Safe love is consistent.
You don't have to guess where you stand.

It is the same on good days and bad ones.

5. Safe love takes responsibility, not control

In unsafe relationships, you carry all the weight.

In safe love:

- both people apologize
- both grow
- both communicate
- both take responsibility
- both show grace

Safe love is shared, not one-sided.

6. Safe love allows you to be imperfect

Unsafe love expects perfection—
and punishes mistakes.

Safe love allows you to:

- learn
- grow
- have emotions
- communicate honestly
- make mistakes
- be human

You do not lose love when you struggle.

7. Safe love looks like the heart of God

God's love is:

- patient
- kind
- protective
- gentle
- truthful
- comforting
- steady

Healthy human love will have the same qualities.

It won't be perfect,
but it will be patterned after God's heart.

Love is not supposed to hurt you.
Love is supposed to *heal you where the world broke you.*

8. You can learn to recognize safe love by the peace it brings

Pay attention to your body:

- If you can breathe around them
- If your shoulders relax
- If you don't have to perform
- If you feel valued
- If you feel seen

- If your nervous system calms
- If you feel closer to God, not further

That is safe love.

Safe love feels like home —
the home you never had,
but always deserved.

Healthy Boundaries Without Fear

For many survivors, boundaries feel dangerous.
Not because boundaries are wrong—
but because in the past, boundaries were met with:

- anger
- guilt trips
- punishment
- manipulation
- silent treatment
- withdrawal
- rejection

So your nervous system learned:

"If I protect myself, I won't get hurt."

But God designed boundaries for your safety, peace,
and dignity.
They are not walls to shut people out—
they are doors that allow love in and keep harm out.

Learning boundaries isn't selfish.
It's healing.

1. Boundaries are not rejection — they are clarity

A boundary is simply saying:

**"This is what I can do.
This is what I cannot do.
This is what I'm comfortable with.
This is what I am not comfortable with."**

It's honesty, not hostility.

You're not pushing people away—
you're inviting them to love you the right way.

2. Healthy boundaries come from knowing your worth

When you grow up feeling small, scared, or invisible,
you learn to accept things that are beneath your value.

But boundaries flow from identity.

When you believe:

**"I am loved by God.
I deserve respect.**

**I deserve safety.
I deserve peace.”**

Boundaries start to feel natural.
Your worth is what strengthens your “no.”

3. You don’t need massive boundaries — just consistent ones

Many survivors feel like they must either:

- sacrifice everything
  OR
- cut everyone off

But real boundaries are steady, not dramatic.

Examples:

- “I can’t talk right now; let’s discuss this tomorrow.”
- “I’m not comfortable with yelling. Let’s continue when we’re calm.”
- “No, I’m not available.”
- “That doesn’t work for me.”
- “I need space when I’m overwhelmed.”

Small boundaries, practiced consistently, change everything.

4. People who love you will respect your boundaries

You'll know someone's heart by how they respond
to your boundaries.

Healthy people respond with:
- understanding
- patience
- respect
- curiosity
- cooperation

Unhealthy people respond with:

- anger
- guilt
- manipulation
- victim-playing
- punishment

Boundaries don't break relationships.
They reveal them.

5. Boundaries don't require explanations

You can simply say:

- "No, thank you."
- "I can't do that."
- "That doesn't work for me."

You don't need:

- long paragraphs

- apologies
- justifications
- excuses

Your "no" is a complete sentence.

6. God equips you to set boundaries without fear

Pray:

"Lord, strengthen me to protect the heart You are healing."

God is not asking you to be harsh.
He is asking you to be wise.

Boundaries are a form of stewardship.
You are protecting a healing heart —
and God honors that.

7. Boundaries will feel uncomfortable at first — but not forever

At first you may feel:

- guilt
- fear
- anxiety
- shakiness
- pressure

That's normal.

Your nervous system is unlearning years of
conditioning.
But the more you set healthy boundaries,
the more you feel:

- peace
- confidence
- clarity
- stability
- self-respect

And others will learn how to love you safely.

8. Boundaries don't push out love — they make room for it

When you protect your heart:

- love becomes healthier
- connections become safer
- peace grows
- emotional chaos shrinks
- God's voice becomes clearer

Boundaries prepare your life
for the love and future God intends for you.

Trusting Again Without Losing Yourself

Trusting again after trauma isn't simple.
Your heart remembers what happened:

- the promises broken

- the manipulation
- the lies
- the abandonment
- the betrayal
- the years you spent giving more than you received

So your heart learned:

"Trusting people means losing myself."

But that isn't true.
That was the pattern of unhealthy people,
not the definition of trust.

Healthy trust does not require losing your identity.
It requires learning how to stay rooted in who you are
while letting someone in at a safe pace.

1. You don't have to trust quickly — only honestly

Trauma often teaches you to trust too fast
or not at all.

But healthy trust happens in the middle:

- slow
- steady
- intentional
- paced
- safe

You don't have to open your whole heart at once.
You can open it piece by piece.
Trust that grows slowly is trust that grows safely.

2. Trust is an invitation, not a surrender

Old wounds make trust feel like:

- losing control
- becoming vulnerable
- letting someone else decide your worth
- handing over your power

But healthy trust is not surrendering yourself.
It is allowing someone to meet you
without abandoning who you are.

You can trust and still:

- speak up
- set boundaries
- say no
- rest in your identity
- honor your needs
- protect your peace

Trusting someone does not erase your voice.
It strengthens it.

3. Trust is earned, not assumed

You no longer need to trust people because:

- they say the right words
- they show quick affection
- they promise change
- they appear confident
- they want connection
- you feel chemistry
- you don't want to be alone

Trust grows through:

- consistency
- reliability
- honesty
- respect
- accountability
- integrity
- emotional safety
- time

People show you who they are over time.
Your heart can learn to wait and watch.

4. You can trust God while learning to trust people

This is the balance that changes everything.

Pray:

**"Lord, guide my discernment.
Help me see clearly.
Protect my heart as I learn to trust again."**

When God leads your relationships,
you trust from wisdom —
not from fear
and not from desperation.

5. Trust never asks you to abandon yourself

If trust feels like:

- ignoring your needs
- staying quiet to keep peace
- shrinking yourself
- abandoning your boundaries
- excusing harmful behavior
- betraying your values

that is not trust.
That is self-abandonment.

Healthy trust leaves room for YOU.

The real you.
The healed you.
The growing you.

6. Trust builds slowly through shared safety

- Watch for these signs:
- your body relaxes around them
- conversations feel safe
- disagreements don't turn into chaos
- you can say "no" without fear
- they listen

- they show up consistently
- they apologize when needed
- they treat your heart with care

When someone makes you feel safe,
your trust grows naturally.

You don't have to force it.

7. You can walk away from anyone who threatens your peace

No explanation needed.
No guilt.
No second guessing.

Trust is a gift,
not an obligation.

If someone mishandles your heart,
you can withdraw trust
and still remain loving, wise, and grounded.

Your heart is valuable.
Not everyone deserves full access to it.

8. You can trust again — and stay whole

Trust after trauma is not about replacing your past.
It's about rewriting your future.

It's learning that:

- you can open your heart without losing it
- you can love without erasing yourself
- you can be vulnerable without being destroyed
- you can lean on God as you choose the people who get close to you
- you can protect your peace and still experience connection

Healing doesn't make your heart guarded—
it makes your heart wise.

You won't lose yourself this time.
You're building a life where love and identity
can finally coexist.

Becoming the Woman You Were Always Meant to Be

Healing is not just about letting go of the past.
It's about stepping into the future God wrote for
you
long before anyone hurt you.

For years, trauma shaped the version of yourself
you felt forced to be:

- quiet
- careful
- hyper-independent
- guarded
- over-giving
- afraid

- self-blaming
- small

But that was survival.

It was not your identity.

Healing brings you back to yourself—
not the wounded version,
but the woman God designed you to be
before the world tried to break her.

1. You are becoming a woman who knows her worth

Not from confidence alone,
but from truth.

You are learning to say:

- "I am loved."
- "I am valuable."
- "I matter."
- "I am worthy of good things."
- "I deserve healthy love."
- "I am a child of God."

When you know your worth,
you stop negotiating with anything beneath it.

2. You are becoming a woman who lives from peace, not fear

Fear once controlled your:

- decisions
- relationships
- reactions
- self-perception
- boundaries

But you are learning to breathe deeper,
pray sooner,
trust God more,
and listen to His voice over your anxiety.

Fear may speak,
but it no longer leads.

3. You are becoming a woman with strong, healthy boundaries

Not because you're cold—
but because you finally understand
that your heart deserves protection.

You are learning to:

- say no without guilt
- take space without apology
- speak honestly
- walk away from what hurts
- stay rooted in your values
- guard your peace

Strength is no longer about surviving chaos
but choosing peace on purpose.

**4. You are becoming a woman who loves
differently**

Not desperately.
Not fearfully.
Not from insecurity or abandonment wounds.

You are learning to love from:

- wholeness
- wisdom
- discernment
- emotional clarity
- spiritual maturity

Your love is becoming a reflection of God's heart,
not the patterns of your past.

**5. You are becoming a woman who trusts God
more deeply**

Not blindly—
but because you've *experienced* Him.

You've seen:
His protection
His guidance
His presence in your darkest moments
His strength in your weakness
His comfort in your grief

His voice in your healing
You're learning that God is not distant.
He is deeply involved
in every part of your restoration.

6. You are becoming a woman who is emotionally safe for herself

This is one of the greatest gifts of healing.

You're learning to be:

- gentle with yourself
- patient with your heart
- honoring of your feelings
- respectful of your needs
- compassionate toward your pain

You no longer abandon yourself.
You no longer silence yourself.
You no longer fight yourself.

You champion yourself.

7. You are becoming a woman with purpose

Your story is no longer a source of shame.
It is a testimony.

Your healing is not only for you—
it will touch others.

You will:

- comfort people through your wisdom
- love people with deeper empathy
- guide others through their pain
- speak truth that sets hearts free
- become a light in places where others still struggle

Nothing you lived was wasted.

God is using every piece of your story
to birth strength, purpose, and calling in you.

8. You are becoming the woman God always knew you could be

Not broken.
Not forgotten.
Not defined by trauma.
Not shaped by your past.

But:

- whole
- wise
- strong
- loved
- redeemed
- restored
- renewed
- victorious

This is who you were **always meant to be**.

And by **God's grace**,
this is who you are becoming.

Every step,
every tear,
every prayer,
every piece of healing
has been leading you here.

To the woman God has always seen in you.

The woman you are now rising into.

To every woman who has carried pain in silence,
to every woman who has survived what should have
broken her,
to every woman who has felt unworthy, unseen, or
unloved—
this message is for you.

You are stronger than you think.
Not because you haven't fallen,
but because **you kept rising** even when you didn't
know how.

You have endured storms that other people will
never understand.
You have survived heartbreaks that tried to destroy
you.
You have lived through nights when your soul felt
like it was collapsing under the weight of your past.
And yet—
here you are.

Still breathing.
Still fighting.
Still hoping.
Still healing.
Still reaching for God's hand.
Still choosing life.

That is **not** weakness.

That is courage.

A Letter From Me to You

My friend,

Before you close this book, I want to say something
from my heart to yours.

I know you're hurt.
I know the kind of pain that lives deep and quiet,
the kind you carry even when you smile.
I know the tiredness that comes from fighting
battles no one else sees.
And I know how heavy it feels to heal while still
trying to hold yourself together.

But I also know your strength.
I've seen the kind of resilience that only comes
from surviving what should have broken you.
I've seen how you keep showing up for life, even
when life hasn't always shown up for you.
And I want you to know—I'm proud of you.

You may not feel strong every day, but strength
isn't loud.
Sometimes it's just getting out of bed.
Sometimes it's choosing to breathe through the
memories.
Sometimes it's whispering a prayer when your heart
feels too tired to speak.

And through every moment, every tear, every step-

God has chosen you.

Not because you are perfect,
but because you are His.
Because He sees the woman you are becoming.
Because He knows the purpose inside you that pain
could not destroy.

Whatever you've walked through,
whatever you're still healing from,
I want you to remember this:

You can get through this.
You can rise from this.
You can come out on top—stronger, softer,
wiser, and more filled with God's love than ever
before.

Your story didn't end in the dark.
You are heading toward a future filled with peace,
safety, and goodness—
the kind of life you have always deserved.

I'm cheering for you.
I'm believing for you.
And I am so grateful that our stories touched for
even a moment. You're not alone, my friend.
You never were.
And you never will be.

With love,

Robin L. O'Brien

AUTHOR BIO

Robin L. O'Brien is a writer, wife, mother, and survivor who believes in the power of truth-telling and stubborn love. After growing up in a world shaped by trauma, loss, and the silence that often follows both, Robin rebuilt her life with courage, faith, and a deep desire to help others feel less alone.

Her lifelong passion is turning painful experiences into pathways of healing—for herself, her family, and anyone who has carried wounds they never chose. When she isn't writing, Robin works in accounting, dreams big entrepreneurial dreams, enjoys dancing with her husband, spending time with her family, and finds her greatest peace in the arms of the man who truly loves her – her husband.

She lives in Missouri, where she continues to write stories that spark hope.

Other Books By Robin L O'Brien

Life's Journey – **A collection of Poems**

www.ingramcontent.com/pod-product-compliance
Lightning Source LLC
Chambersburg PA
CBHW061448150726
47987CB00001B/376